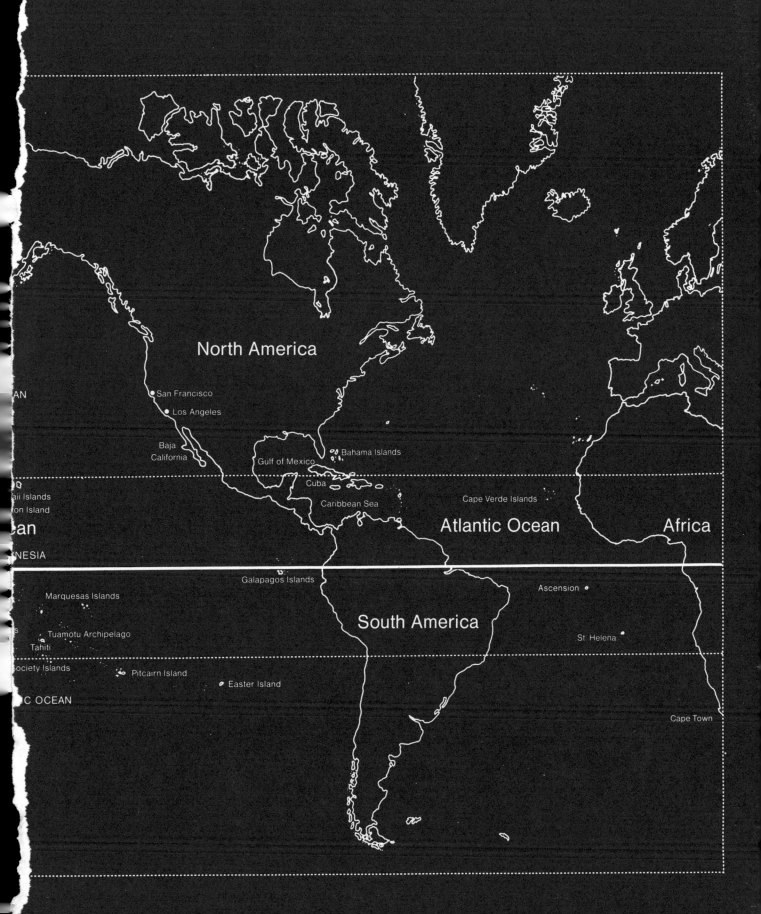

North America

AN

● San Francisco

● Los Angeles

Baja
California

Gulf of Mexico

Cuba

●● Bahama Islands

Cape Verde Islands

Atlantic Ocean

Africa

Caribbean Sea

ii Islands
on Island

an

NESIA

Galapagos Islands

Ascension ●

Marquesas Islands

South America

St. Helena ●

Tuamotu Archipelago
Tahiti

Society Islands

Pitcairn Island

Easter Island

C OCEAN

Cape Town

Jacket photos

top left: *Holacanthus passer,* photo: Roediger
top right: *Chaetodon xanthurus,* photo: Nieuwenhuizen
bottom photo: *Holacanthus clarionensis,* photo: Friese

This book is dedicated to Dr. William A. Gosline, who
helped guide me toward an ichthyological career
and generously gave me a large portion of his
personal library on his retirement from the University
of Hawaii.

Library of Congress Cataloging in Publication Data (Revised)

Steene, Roger C
  Butterfly and angelfishes of the world.

  "A Wiley-Interscience publication".
  Vol. 2 by G. R. Allen.
  Bibliography: p.
  Includes indexes.
  CONTENTS: v. I. Australia.
  1. Chaetodontidae. 2. Pomacanthidae. 3. Marine
aquarium fishes. I. Allen, Gerald R. II. Title.
  QL638.C48S74   1978   597'.58   78-17351
  ISBN 0-471-05618-9 (v. 2)

© Copyright 1979 MERGUS Publishers Hans A. Baensch · Melle · W. Germany

Artwork: H. J. Braun, Grafic Design Studio, Werther, W. Germany
Typesetting: Fotosatz F. Nollmann, Werther, W. Germany
Printing: MERGUS Press, Hongkong
Editor: Hans A. Baensch, Melle, W. Germany
First Edition in English 1980

Printed in Hongkong

Dr. Gerald R. Allen

Butterfly and Angelfishes of the World

Volume 2

**Atlantic Ocean
Caribbean Sea
Red Sea
Indo-Pacific**

Together
With Volume 1
All The Species
Of The World
Are Described

Including
300 Color
Illustrations
With More Than
150 Original
Underwater
Photos

With The
Assistance Of
Hans A. Baensch

Foreword
Prof. Dr.
Konrad Lorenz

**A WILEY-INTERSCIENCE PUBLICATION
JOHN WILEY & SONS, New York · Toronto**

Contents

Foreword

by Konrad Z. Lorenz, Altenberg

Gerald R. Allen is one of the few scientists who uses both observations of animals in their natural habitats and studies of live animals in captivity as sources of knowledge. Among ichthyologists especially, it seems common for divers to show a certain disdain for aquarium lovers and, on the other hand, relatively few aquarium keepers have dived in the open sea. When an aquarium keeper or other animal owner understands how to provide natural and biologically correct living conditions, insofar as this is possible for the animals involved, the study of captive animals has a major advantage over the study of free-living ones: one is then in a position to see, *side by side,* related species which normally are found in widely separated locations, and this stimulates one to make comparisons and to consider their taxonomic relationships. Important discoveries have been made this way. Oskar Heinroth and Charles Otis Whitman, the great pioneers of comparative animal behavior, were both "animal lovers" who studied many related species of birds in captivity or semi-captivity: Whitman studied pigeons, and Heinroth ducks. I, the writer of this foreword, have studied both ducks, as did Heinroth, and cichlid fishes, which were no less decisive in my thinking. From them my interest gradually extended to the entire large group of spiny-finned fish, the *Acanthopterygii.* This group of fishes, with its rich variety of forms, gives aquarists the opportunity to contribute to comparative biology through their observation.

The spiny-finned fish, and especially the perchlike fish *(Percomorphae),* are particularly interesting and rich in information for taxonomists because, having first evolved in a comparatively recent geological age – near the beginning of the Tertiary – they have since branched into innumerable families, genera and species with astounding biological success, and have come to occupy seemingly all suitable ecological niches accessible to fish.

Groups such as these, which include an especially large number of genera and species, are very attractive to the comparative biologist, whether morphologist or behaviorist. The cichlids and damselfishes *(Pomacentridae)* are one such group, and the butterflyfishes *(Chaetodontidae)* and angelfishes *(Pomacanthidae)* are another. Gerald R. Allen, who has also worked with the *Pomacentridae,* has devoted this book to the latter group of fish, thus completing Roger C. Steene's already published volume.

One particularly notable thing about Allen is his "taxonomic intuition". This no doubt comes from his profound knowledge of the fish species he has dealt with, a knowledge which stems not from underwater observations or aquarium studies alone but from the use of both approaches.

The relationship between the *Pomacanthidae* and *Chaetodontidae* has only been recently clarified by Warren Burgess, who has shown convincingly that these families are not as closely related as was originally thought. In the Chaetodontidae, the development of the larvae is characterized by the so-called *Tholichthys* stage, while the Pomacanthidae have nothing comparable to this. The taxonomic relationships within these two families remain mostly unknown. In this book, Allen has followed Burgess' subfamily classification in grouping the various butterflyfishes and that of Shen and Liu for the angelfishes.

Scientists have very seldom collected as much knowledge about a group of animals as Allen and Steene have assembled in these two volumes about butterfly and angelfishes. They have set themselves the ambitious task of describing all of the species known to date. They have observed most of the species themselves in their natural habitat and have also kept many species in aquaria. Thus they are particularly qualified to describe both the ecology and the requirements for aquarium care of these fishes.

In a time in which most people's thinking is becoming alienated from Nature in a very harmful way, it is encouraging to see an obvious steady increase in interest in marine animals and their care in saltwater aquaria. Both the care of marine fish and their scientific observation under natural conditions induce sensitivity and biological "intuition" in the aquarium owner and a faculty for observation in the diver interested in fish. Aquarium keeping and underwater observation are not "hobbies" in the usual sense, but rather serious occupations which require full participation. Thus they are a "school" of general enjoyment of life whose educational value cannot be treasured enough.

This book about the butterfly and angelfishes, whose beauty is enchanting indeed, will definitely help more people find access to this "school" and experience the fascination of Nature with observant eyes and open hearts.

Konrad Z. Lorenz
Altenberg, Austria
July, 1978

Foreword from the Author

This book represents the second volume of a two-part set that covers the butterflyfishes and angelfishes of the world. Species inhabiting the Australia–New Guinea region were featured in Volume 1 which was written by my good friend Roger C. Steene. This was an appropriate starting point, for there are more butterflyfishes and angelfishes in that region than in any other part of the world. In this volume the remaining species of the world are described. The result is a fully comprehensive treatment of these popular fishes.

Perhaps no other group of tropical marine fishes has captured man's fancy to the same degree as the butterflyfishes and angelfishes. Certainly they must be included among the most beautiful and graceful of all creatures of the sea. Nature has spared no expense in lavishing a tremendous wealth of colorful and bizarre patterns. Thus it is not surprising that these fishes have attracted a great deal of attention over the last 200 to 300 years, first as objects of scientific curiosity and more recently as aquarium pets and a favorite subject of photographers. Indeed, perhaps no other fish groups have commanded so much popular attention in recent times. The butterflyfishes and angelfishes seem to epitomize the unique beauty of a tropical coral reef and have been featured in numerous articles and photographic essays.

The two volumes in this series represent the first comprehensive treatment of the combined Chaetodontidae-Pomacanthidae. These two families are closely allied and until just a few years ago were usually considered as subfamilies of the Chaetodontidae. Volume 2 features 65 chaetodontids and 43 pomacanthids, in addition to five species that are also discussed in Volume 1. Therefore our total coverage for both volumes encompasses all the world's species, 114 butterflyfishes and 74 angelfishes, many of which are illustrated for the first time, often with superb underwater photographs taken in the natural habitat. General information, which deals with classification, natural history, and aquarium maintenance, is also given. Another section covers the fascinating subject of hybridization which appears to be a common phenomenon among these fishes. The extensive bibliography that appears at the end of the book will prove useful to scientists as well as amateur naturalists.

In summary, this volume and Volume 1, which are designed to serve as a practical and informative guide to the butterflyfishes and angelfishes of the world, will allow even an aquarium novice or beginning student of ichthyology to gain an immediate expertise in the classification and biology of these groups.

Acknowledgments

I offer my sincere thanks to Mr. Roger C. Steene and Mr. Hans A. Baensch, publisher, for inviting me to participate in this project. I am also grateful to Dr. Konrad Lorenz, who generously offered to write the foreword. Dr. Walter A. Starck II made it possible for me to make extensive observations on the butterflyfishes and angelfishes of the Palau Islands and the Melanesian Archipelago while cruising aboard his research vessel *El Torito* in 1970–1973. The National Geographic Society, Washington, D. C., funded expeditions to Easter Island (1969), Lord Howe Island (1973), and the Solomon Islands (1973). Several people were instrumental in providing assistance during a world tour in 1975–1976 on which butterflyfishes and angelfishes were observed and photographed in their natural habitat: Dr. Patrick Colin (Puerto Rico), Dr. George De Bruin (Sri Lanka), Mr. David Fridman (Eilat, Red Sea), Mr. Jack Moyer (Japan), and Dr. Ross Robertson (Panama). The Smithsonian Tropical Research Institute made their facilities available at their Panama field stations on this same trip. Thanks are also due the Food and Agricultural Organization (F.A.O.) of the United Nations and Dr. Walter Fischer of the same organization for making possible observations and collections in the Persian Gulf, Gulf of Oman, and central Red Sea in 1977. On this expedition Dr. Peter Vine and his wife Paula were particularly helpful during a visit to Jeddah, Saudi Arabia, and Dr. William F. Smith-Vaniz assisted with diving activities. I am especially grateful to the Western Australian Museum for supporting fieldwork and various research projects during the last four years. The Australian National Parks and Wildlife Service under the auspices of Mr. Vance Russell, provided funds for a visit to Christmas Island, Indian Ocean in May–June 1978. Mr. Roger Lubbock and Mr. Alan Power were especially helpful in providing photographs of relatively rare species. I am also indebted to the photographers and to Mr. Chlupaty for giving hints on aquarium maintenance. Mr. Martin Thompson of Perth prepared the many valuable paintings that are featured in this volume. I am extremely grateful to Dr. John E. Randall of the Bernice P. Bishop Museum in Honolulu, who served as my Ph. D. chairman at the University of Hawaii. Dr. Randall, or "Jack" as he is known to his colleagues around the world, provided much of the original inspiration for my interest in coral reef fishes and continues to aid my research in numerous and invaluable ways; for example, during the present study he provided photographs of species from remote areas and accompanied me on numerous field trips. I am also grateful to Dr. Warren E. Burgess whose study of the butterflyfishes aroused my own interest in this group during our years together as graduate students at the University of Hawaii. Dr. Burgess' study is referred to throughout this book. Finally, I thank my wife Connie Allen for her continuing encouragement and moral support. She also did an excellent job of preparing the typescript.

Gerald R. Allen, Perth, Australia, 1978

External Body Structure of the Butterflyfishes and Angelfishes

The external features of a typical butterflyfish are listed below. In addition, the heads of several representative angelfishes are compared. The following abbreviations are used in the drawings:

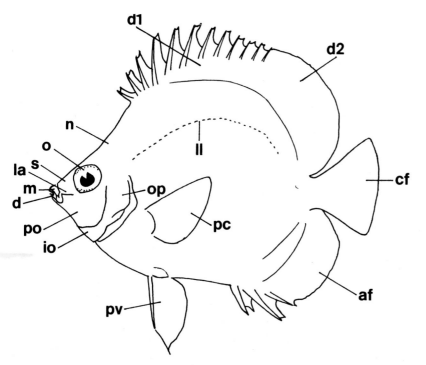

af = anal fin
cf = caudal fin
ct = scale ctenii (microscopic spines on scale edges)
d = dentary (lower jaw)
d_1 = spinous or first dorsal fin
d_2 = soft or second dorsal fin
io = interopercle bone
la = lacrymal or preorbital bone
ll = lateral line
m = maxillary (upper jaw)
n = nape (forehead)
o = orbit (eye)
op = opercle bone
pc = pectoral fin
po = preopercle bone (cheek)
ps = preopercle spine
pv = pelvic fin
sf = scale focus

SL – standard length – this measurement is the distance between the tip of the snout and the base of the tail.
TL – total length – is seldom used by ichthyologists working with museum specimens, because portions of the tail are frequently missing or damaged.

Pomacanthus scale   ct / sf   **Holacanthus scale**

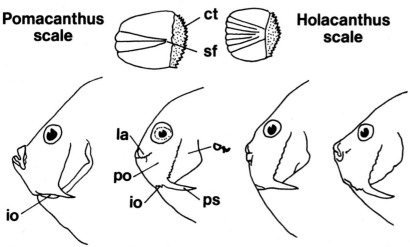

Pomacanthus Centropyge Apolemichthys Pygoplites

214.
A small school of *Heniochus intermedius* with a pair of *Chaetodon austriacus* in the background.
Underwater photo from the Red Sea.
Photo: Moosleitner.

Family
Chaetodontidae   Butterflyfishes

Introduction

The butterflyfishes of the family *Chaetodontidae* are renowned for their striking color patterns, delicate shapes, and graceful swimming movements. For most divers and aquarists they head the list of favorite fishes. This family contains 114 species which occur mainly in tropical seas around coral reefs, although a few are distributed in cooler, temperate waters. Most of the species dwell in depths of less than 20 meters (66 ft), but some are restricted to deep water down to at least 200 meters (656 ft). Juveniles often undergo color transformations with growth, but these changes are far less spectacular than those observed in some of the angelfishes. Young specimens are highly prized as aquarium fishes and are frequently imported to Europe and America, particularly from the Orient.

Zoogeography

Butterflyfishes occur in all tropical seas and a small number are found in cool, temperate regions. The vast Indo-Pacific faunal province is the home of nearly 90% of the species. The remaining 12 species dwell in the tropical Atlantic Ocean. Many have relatively wide distributions: about 25 butterflyfishes occur in the western Pacific and the Indian oceans. Other species have more restricted ranges, although some may be fairly substantial: for example, the entire western Indian Ocean or a large portion of the Pacific. Two regions are noteworthy because of their high percentage of endemism (i. e. species that occur in those regions and nowhere else), the first of which is the Red Sea and adjacent Gulf of Aden where seven endemic species are present. The other is the Hawaiian Islands where four endemics occur. Five butterflyfishes have extremely restricted distributions: *Amphichaetodon melbae* (San Felix Island), *Chaetodon declivis* (Fatu Hiva, Marquesas Islands), *C. guezei* (Réunion), *C. litus* (Easter Island), and *Hemitaurichthys multispinosus* (Pitcairn Island). The following five areas have the richest butterflyfish faunas in the world (number of species indicated in parentheses): 1. Australia (50); 2. Philippine Islands (45); 3. Indonesia (44); 4. Taiwan (43) and 5. New Guinea (42). The table that follows below gives an approximate zoogeographic analysis of the family. The subregion categories listed under each major region are mutually exclusive (i. e. a particular species is not included in more than one subregion).

Zoogeography of the Butterflyfishes

Region	Subregion	No. species restricted to region
Indo-West Pacific		
	Wide-ranging over most of the area	20
	Widespread W. Pacific	15
	W. Indian Ocean	9
	Australia and offshore islands	8
	Indo-Australian Archipelago to Japan	9
	W. Pacific-E. Indian Ocean	8
	Red Sea	7
	Widespread Indian Ocean	6
	S. E. Oceania	5
	Hawaiian Islands	4
	East Indies	2
	Central and E. Indian Ocean	2
	Gulf of Oman-Persian Gulf	2
	Southern W. Pacific	1
Eastern Pacific		4
Atlantic		
	W. Atlantic	7
	Central and E. Atlantic	5

Biology

Butterflyfishes are conspicuous on all tropical reefs. Most species are found in extensive areas of live coral in relatively shallow water less than 15 – 20 m (49 – 66 ft), which reflects their dependence on coral as a source of nourishment and shelter. A small number of species, such as *Chelmon mülleri* of northern Australia inhabit silty coastal reefs where coral diversity is low. Others, like *Chaetodon mitratus* of the Indian Ocean, inhabit rubble areas or deep water slopes where there is little or no coral, and a few species, for example *Hemitaurichthys polylepis*, form aggregations high above the bottom where they forage on zooplankton.

Chaetodontids are mainly "home-ranging" diurnal fishes (see Reese, 1973 and 1975). In other words, most species are confined to isolated patch reefs or relatively small areas of more extensive reef system. They travel extensively throughout the range, foraging for food. A small number of species, including *Chaetodon trifascialis, C. baronessa, C. triangulum,* and *C. larvatus,* are territorial: they inhabit areas that contain one or more large heads of plate coral *(Acropora)* and cover several square meters. These territories are defended vigorously against members of the same species and other coral-feeding butterflyfishes. In most other species both inter- and intraspecific agonistic (fighting, chasing, fleeing) encounters are generally infrequent. Ehrlich *et. al.* (1977), however, found that a significant amount of fighting and minor squabbling does take place at dusk and dawn in defense of night resting places. At dusk all foraging activities terminate rather abruptly and the fishes retreat to crevices or coral heads where they remain motionless until morning. Many species assume a special nocturnal coloration that frequently consists of general bleaching of the overall pattern or darkening of the dorsal portion of the body with one or two pale spots in this region (see Fig. 65, Vol. 1). Some species, such as *Chaetodon trifasciatus, C. plebeius,* and *C. aureofasciatus* apparently return to the same "roosting" places each night, whereas others seek shelter at the end of the day in any suitable site in the immediate vicinity.

A great deal of controversy has centered on the possible reasons for the bright color patterns of coral reef fishes, particularly the butterflyfishes and angelfishes. The famous biologist Professor Konrad Lorenz has suggested that the "poster" colorations of reef fishes act as intraspecific sign stimuli that serve to space individuals and result in ample food resources for all, thus preventing unnecessary aggression between noncompeting fish of different kinds. Ehrlich *et al.* (1977), however, disagree with this idea on the basis of field observations conducted on the Great Barrier Reef at Lizard Island. They believe that color has little to do with territoriality and suggest that the patterns probably have several functions, such as communication during courtship and breeding, the avoidance of predators by signaling distasteful or unpleasant (i. e., bones and sharp spines) qualities, and others that remain undetermined.

Reese (1975) studied the social behavior of butterflyfishes and found several basic patterns. Some species, including the territorial ones mentioned, are usually solitary or on occasion form small groups. Others are normally pair forming and, depending on the frequency of their pairing tendencies, are termed weakly or strongly pairing. The weak category includes such species as *Chaetodon citrinellus, C. lunula, C. ornatissimus, C. quadrimaculatus,* and *C. reticulatus.* Examples of strongly pairing species are *C. ephippium, C. multicinctus, C. punctatofasciatus, C. triangulum, C. trifasciatus, C. unimaculatus,* and *C. vagabundus.* Reese conducted most of this study at Enewetak Atoll and on the southern Great Barrier Reef. He emphasized that certain species may exhibit different social behavior at different localities. Another type of social structure found in some species, and one that was not investigated by Reese, is the formation of large aggregations that may number as many as several hundred individuals. This phenomenon is found in some of the species of *Hemitaurichthys* and in a few *Chaetodon* such as *C. miliaris.* Little information is available on the reproductive behavior of butterflyfishes. About all that is clear is that they produce tiny, buoyant eggs that float to the surface after their release. The hatching time is probably similar to that of angelfishes (18 – 30 hours at about 29° C [84° F]). The larvae known as *Tholichthys* are covered with bony plates and are pelagic for periods ranging from a few weeks to several months.

The general feeding habits of butterflyfishes have been determined in studies by Hiatt and Strasburg (1960), Randall (1967), Reese (1975), and Anderson *et al.* (in press). There appear to be five main feeding types in the family, based on dietary items found among the gut contents and from underwater observations of feeding behavior. Species closely associated with rich coral areas, such as *Chaetodon trifasciatus, C. trifascialis, C. baronessa, C. triangulum, C. plebeius,* and *C. ornatissimus,* feed on hard or stony corals. A second group, which includes *C. lineolatus, C. melannotus,* and *C. unimaculatus,* feeds mainly on soft corals, although a significant amount of hard corals may be eaten as well. A third category includes species that feed on small benthic invertebrates (excluding corals), particularly polychaete worms and small crustaceans. This group contains *C. auriga, Chelmon rostratus, Chaetodon sedentarius, C. striatus,* and the species of *Forcipiger.* A fourth group depends largely on zooplankton for its nourishment; examples are *Hemitaurichthys polylepis, H. zoster,* and *Heniochus diphreutes.* The last major category contains opportunistic omnivores or generalists that feed on a wide range of items from the above categories as well as algae.

Taxonomy
Classification of the butterflyfishes in this book closely follows the Burgess monograph (1978), which is the first truly comprehensive work on this group since Ahl's 1923 publication. I have sometimes followed Burgess rather than my own convictions mainly for the sake of uniformity; for example, it is my opinion that a strong case can be made for the retention of the genera *Megaprotodon* and *Gonochaetodon,* both considered subgenera of *Chaetodon* by Burgess. In any case, the decision to recognize genera versus subgenera appears to be largely subjective and it seems more important at this stage to strive for uniformity . Because of their distinctive shapes and color patterns, butterflyfishes are relatively easy to identify. The only species-related problems presented by the group concern slight color pattern variations that occur in some forms and are correlated with geography. Again, I have followed Burgess in the few cases in which problems of this

nature have developed. However, I consider some of these species to be on rather shaky ground, and when additional specimens and facts about their distribution become known they may prove to be invalid. Instead they may just be color variants of a single species. Examples involve the following species pairs: *C. hoefleri – C. marleyi, C. melannotus – C. ocellicaudus, C. baronessa – C. triangulum,* and *C. mertensii – C. madagascariensis.* Burgess also recognized Pacific and Indian Ocean subspecies for *C. trifasciatus* and *C. unimaculatus.* The classification of the species within the different subgenera is shown in the following pages.

214a. (lower photo)
C. trifasciatus
from the Pacific
Ocean.
Photo: Steene.

214b. (upper photo)
C. trifasciatus
from the Indian
Ocean.
Photo: Steene.

FAMILY CHAETODONTIDAE – 114 species

Genus *Amphichaetodon* –
2 species (S. Pacific)

Genus *Chaetodon*
Subgenus *Chaetodon* –
28 species (circumtropical)
Subgenus *Chaetodontops* –
9 species (Indo-West Pacific)
Subgenus *Citharoedus* –
2 species (Indo-West Pacific)
Subgenus *Corallochaetodon* –
3 species (Indo-West Pacific)
Subgenus *Discochaetodon* –
4 species (Indo-Australian Archipelago)
Subgenus *Gonochaetodon* –
3 species (Indo-West Pacific)
Subgenus *Lepidochaetodon* –
1 species (Indo-West Pacific)
Subgenus *Megaprotodon* –
1 species (Indo-West Pacific)
Subgenus *Prognathodes* –
7 species (E. Pacific, Atlantic, and W. Ind. Ocean).
Subgenus *Radophorus* –
16 species (Indo-West Pacific)
Subgenus *Rhombochaetodon* –
5 species (Indo-West Pacific)
Subgenus *Roa* –
6 species (Indo-West Pacific)
Subgenus *Tetrachaetodon* –
4 species (Indo-West Pacific)

Genus *Chelmon* –
3 species (Indo-Australian Archipelago)

Genus *Chelmonops* –
1 species (S. Australia)

Genus *Coradion* –
3 species (far W. Pacific)

Genus *Forcipiger* –
2 species (Indo-Pacific)

Genus *Hemitaurichthys* –
4 species (Indo-West Pacific)

Genus *Heniochus* –
8 species (Indo-West Pacific)

Genus *Johnrandallia* –
1 species (E. Pacific)

Genus *Parachaetodon* –
1 species (Indo-West Pacific)

The Species of Butterflyfishes, Family *Chaetodontidae* (Summary of Volumes 1 and 2)

The following list is based largely on Burgess (1978). Valid species appear in boldface type, synonyms in italics. The species name is followed by the author and the approximate geographic distribution is given for valid species. Page numbers refer to Volumes 1 and 2 of **Butterfly and Angelfishes.** The main features that characterize the genera and subgenera are outlined briefly.

Genus *Amphichaetodon* Burgess, 1978

Dorsal spines 12; dorsal fin triangular; lateral line complete with 47–55 scales; snout moderate, 2.4–3.3 in length of head; lacrymal bone scaled.

Amphichaetodon howensis (Waite, 1903) – N. Tasman Sea and Lord Howe Island, Vol. 1, p. 59

Amphichaetodon melbae Burgess and Caldwell, 1978 – Isla San Felix, Vol. 2, p. 164

Genus *Chaetodon* Linnaeus, 1758

Dorsal spines 11 to 16; dorsal fin variable in shape; lateral line incomplete with 22–55 scales; snout variable, 1.9–4.5 in length of head; scalation of lacrymal bone variable.

Subgenus *Chaetodon*

Dorsal rays XI–XIV, 18–25; anal rays III, 16–19; rear edge of dorsal and anal fins with blunt angles; snout short, pointed, 2.7–3.3 in length of head; lacrymal bone free and smooth; lateral line in a high arc; scales variable in shape, rounded to angular.

Chaetodon assarius Waite, 1905 – W. Australia, Vol. 1, p. 13

Chaetodon blackburnii Desjardins, 1836 – E. Africa, Vol. 2, p. 171

Chaetodon capistratus Linnaeus, 1758 – W. Atlantic, Vol. 2, p. 173
  Chaetodon bricei Smith, 1897

Chaetodon citrinellus Cuvier, 1831 – Indo-West Pacific, Vol. 1, p. 20
  Chaetodon nigripes De Vis, 1885
  Chaetodon citrinellus var. *semipunctatus* Ahl, 1923

Chaetodon daedalma Jordan and Fowler, 1923 – Japan to Taiwan, Vol. 2, p. 176

Chaetodon dolosus Ahl, 1923 – E. Africa, Vol. 2, p. 181
  Chaetodon mendoncae Smith, 1953

Chaetodon fremblii Bennett, 1828 – Hawaiian Islands, Vol. 2, p. 186
  Chaetodon frehmlii Cuvier, 1831
  Chaetodon bleekeri Seale, 1902

Chaetodon güntheri Ahl, 1923 – S. Japan to Australia, Vol. 1, p. 23

Chaetodon guttatissimus Bennett, 1832 – Indian Ocean and Red Sea, Vol. 2, p. 189
  Chaetodon maculatus Sauvage, 1891

Chaetodon hoefleri Steindachner, 1881 – W. Africa, Vol. 2, p. 191

Chaetodon humeralis Günther, 1860 – E. Pacific, Vol. 2, p. 192

Chaetodon kleinii Bloch, 1790 – Indo-West Pacific – Vol. 1, p. 24
  Chaetodon melastomus Schneider, 1801
  Chaetodon melammystax Schneider, 1801
  Chaetodon virescens Cuvier, 1831
  Chaetodon flavescens Bennett, 1831
  Chaetodon bellulus Thiollière, 1857
  Chaetodon corallicola Snyder, 1904
  Chaetodon cingulatus Fowler, 1934

Chaetodon litus Randall and Caldwell, 1976 – Easter Island, Vol. 2, p. 195

Chaetodon marleyi Regan, 1921 – S. Africa, Vol. 2, p. 199

Chaetodon melannotus Schneider, 1801 – Indo-West Pacific, Vol. 1, p. 28
  Chaetodon dorsalis Rüppell, 1828
  Chaetodon marginatus Cuvier, 1831
  Chaetodon reinwardti Günther, 1860

Chaetodon miliaris Quoy and Gaimard, 1824 – Hawaiian Islands, Vol. 2, p. 204
  Chaetodon mantelliger Jenkins, 1901

Chaetodon multicinctus Garrett, 1863 – Hawaiian Islands, Vol. 2, p. 209

Chaetodon ocellatus Bloch, 1781 – W. Atlantic, Vol. 2, p. 212

Chaetodon bimaculatus Bloch, 1790
Sarothrodus maculo-cinctus Gill, 1861
Sarothrodus ataeniatus Poey, 1868
Sarathrodus amplexicollis Poey, 1875

Chaetodon ocellicaudus Cuvier, 1831 – East Indies to Africa, Vol. 2, p. 214

Chaetodon pelewensis Kner, 1868 – W. Pacific, Vol. 1, p. 34

Chaetodon germanus De Vis, 1884

Chaetodon punctatofasciatus Cuvier, 1831 W. Pacific, Vol. 1, p. 36

Chaetodon punctato-lineatus Gray, 1854

Chaetodon quadrimaculatus Gray, 1831 – W. Pacific, Vol. 2, p. 218

Chaetodon robustus Günther, 1860 – W. Africa, Vol. 2, p. 219

Chaetodon luciae Rochebrune, 1880

Chaetodon sanctaehelenae Günther, 1868 – Ascension and St. Helena islands, Vol. 2, p. 220

Chaetodon sanctaehelenae var. *uniformis* Ahl, 1923

Chaetodon sedentarius Poey, 1858 – W. Atlantic, Vol. 2, p. 222

Chaetodon gracilis Günther, 1860

Chaetodon smithi Randall, 1975 – Pitcairn and Rapa islands, Vol. 2, p. 226

Chaetodon hemichrysurus Burgess and Randall, 1978

Chaetodon striatus Linnaeus, 1758 – W. Atlantic, Vol. 2, p. 228

Chaetodon consuelae Mowbray, 1928
Anisochaetodon trivirgatus Weber and de Beaufort, 1936
Chaetodon striatus var. *albipinnis* Ahl, 1923
Chaetodon striatus var. *dorsimacula* Ahl, 1923

Chaetodon trichrous Günther, 1874 – Society Islands and Tuamotus, Vol. 2, p. 232

Subgenus *Chaetodontops*

Dorsal rays XII, 23–26; anal rays III, 17–22; rear edge of dorsal and anal fins with blunt angles; snout short, 2.8–3.5 in length of head; lateral line in a high, angular arc; lacrymal free and rounded; teeth normal; scales rounded.

Chaetodon adiergastos Seale, 1910 – Philippines to W. Australia, Vol. 1, p. 12

Chaetodon auripes Jordan and Snyder, 1901 – Taiwan to Japan, Vol. 2, p. 168

Chaetodon aureus Temminck and Schlegel, 1842
Chaetodon fallax Ahl, 1923
Chaetodon dorsiocellatus Ahl, 1923

Chaetodon collare Bloch, 1787 – far W. Pacific and Indian Ocean, Vol. 2, p. 174

Chaetodon viridis Bleeker, 1854
Chaetodon praetextatus Cantor, 1850
Chaetodon collare var. *parallelus* Ahl, 1923
Chaetodon fowleri Klausewitz, 1955

Chaetodon fasciatus Forsskål, 1775 – Red Sea, Vol. 2, p. 184

Chaetodon flavus Schneider, 1801

Chaetodon flavirostris Günther, 1874 – S. W. Pacific, Vol. 1, p. 22

Chaetodon aphrodite Ogilby, 1889

Chaetodon lunula (Lacépède, 1803) – Indo-West Pacific, Vol. 1, p. 26

Chaetodon biocellatus Cuvier, 1831

Chaetodon reticulatus Cuvier, 1831 – W. Pacific, Vol. 1, p. 40

Chaetodon superbus Cuvier, 1831

Chaetodon semilarvatus Cuvier, 1831 – Red Sea, Vol. 2, p. 223

Chaetodon melanopoma Playfair, 1866

Chaetodon wiebeli Kaup, 1863 – E. Indies to Japan, Vol. 2, p. 234

Chaetodon bella-maris Seale, 1914
Chaetodon collare var. *kneri* Ahl, 1923
Chaetodon frenatus Fowler, 1934

Subgenus *Citharoedus*

Dorsal rays XII, 23–28; anal rays III, 19–23; spinous dorsal fin evenly graduated, soft portion of dorsal and anal with blunt angle posteriorly: snout short, 3.0–4.0 in length of head; lateral line arc high and angular; teeth in undefined rows at front of jaws; supraorbital horns present in Tholichthys larval stage.

Chaetodon meyeri Schneider, 1801 – Indo-West-Pacific, Vol. 1, p. 31

Holacanthus flavo-niger Lacépède, 1802

Chaetodon ornatissimus Cuvier, 1831 – Indo-West-Pacific, Vol. 1, p. 33

Chaetodon ornatus Gray, 1831
Chaetodon ornatissimus var. *kaupi* Ahl, 1923
Chaetodon lydiae Curtiss, 1938

Subgenus *Corallochaetodon*

Dorsal rays XIII, 20–21; anal rays III, 19; spinous dorsal fin evenly graduated, soft portion of dorsal and anal with rounded angle posteriorly; snout short,

3.1–4.1 in length of head; lateral line in a high, angular arc; teeth grouped in undefined rows at front of jaws; lacrymal almost completely hidden by scales; scales vertically elongate.

Chaetodon austriacus Rüpell, 1835 – Red Sea, Vol. 2, p. 169
>*Chaetodon vittatus* Klunzinger, 1870
>*Chaetodon klunzingeri* Kossman and Räuber, 1876

Chaetodon melapterus Guichenot, 1862 – Persian Gulf and W. Indian Ocean, Vol. 2, p. 200
>*Chaetodon melanopterus* Playfair, 1865
>*Chaetodon trifasciatus* var. *arabica* Steindachner, 1902
>*Chaetodon arabicus* Steindachner, 1903

Chaetodon trifasciatus Park, 1797 – Indo-West-Pacific, Vol. 1, p. 48; Vol. 2, p. 157
>*Chaetodon vittatus* Bloch and Schneider, 1801
>*Chaetodon lunulatus* Quoy and Gaimard, 1824
>*Chaetodon tau-nigrum* Cuvier, 1831
>*Chaetodon bellus* Lay and Bennett, 1839
>*Chaetodon layardi* Blyth, 1852
>*Chaetodon ovalis* Thiollière, 1857
>*Chaetodon pepek* Thiollière, 1857
>*Chaetodon trifasciatus caudifasciatus* Ahl, 1923

Subgenus *Discochaetodon*

Dorsal rays XI, 19–22; anal rays III, 16–18; dorsal and anal fins strongly rounded; snout short, 2.8–4.5 in length of head; lateral line in a low, smooth arc; lacrymal restricted; scales rounded.

Chaetodon aureofasciatus Macleay, 1878 – N. Australia and New Guinea, Vol. 1, p. 14

Chaetodon octofasciatus Bloch, 1787 far W. Pacific, Vol. 1, p. 32
>*Chaetodon octolineatus* Gray, 1854

Chaetodon rainfordi McCulloch, 1923 – E. Australia, Vol. 1, p. 39

Chaetodon tricinctus Waite, 1901 – Norfolk and Lord Howe islands, Vol. 1, p. 46

Subgenus *Gonochaetodon*

Dorsal rays XI, 24–25; anal rays III, 20–22; dorsal fin elevated, spines increasing in length posteriorly; lateral line in a moderately smooth arc; lacrymal free and smooth; scales rhomboid, arranged in a chevron pattern.

Chaetodon baronessa Cuvier, 1831 – W. Pacific, Vol. 1, p. 16

Chaetodon larvatus Cuvier, 1831 – Red Sea, Vol. 2, p. 193
>*Chaetodon karraf* Cuvier, 1831

Chaetodon triangulum Cuvier, 1831 – Indian Ocean, Vol. 2, p. 231

Subgenus *Lepidochaetodon*

Dorsal rays XIII, 21–22; anal rays III, 19; dorsal and anal fins rounded; snout short, 2.5–3.2 in length of head; lateral line in a high, smooth arc; lacrymal partly hidden; teeth in regular rows, the outermost strongest.

Chaetodon unimaculatus Bloch, 1787 – Indo-West-Pacific, Vol. 1, p. 51; Vol. 2, p. 233
>*Chaetodon sphenospilus* Jenkins, 1901
>*Chaetodon unimaculatus interruptus* Ahl, 1923

Subgenus *Megaprotodon*

Dorsal rays XIV, 15; anal rays IV, 15; spinous dorsal fin rounded, spines increasing in length to 5th spine; soft portion of dorsal and anal fins pointed; lateral line in a low arc; scales rhomboid, arranged in a chevron pattern.

Chaetodon trifascialis Quoy and Gaimard, 1824 – Indo-West Pacific, Vol. 1, p. 47
>*Chaetodon strianguli* Gmelin, 1789
>*Chaetodon bifascialis* Cuvier, 1829
>*Chaetodon leachii* Cuvier, 1831
>*Eteira taunayi* Kaup, 1860
>**Megaprotodon striangulus* Bleeker, 1876
>**Megaprotodon trifascialis* Jordan and Seale, 1906
>*Chaetodon tearlachi* Curtiss, 1938

Subgenus *Prognathodes*

Dorsal rays XIII, 18–20; anal rays III, 15–16; spinous dorsal with triangular shape, 3rd or 4th spine the longest; 2nd anal spine significantly longer than 3rd; dorsal fin notched, with rear edge of dorsal and anal fins approximately vertical; snout projecting, 2.1–2.9 in length of head; eye band absent or angled anteriorly below eye; scaly sheath at base of dorsal fin low.

Chaetodon aculeatus (Poey, 1860) – W. Atlantic, Vol. 2, p. 165
>*Chelmo pelta* Günther, 1860
>**Prognathodes aculeatus* Poey, 1868
>*Chaetodon unicolor* Sauvage, 1880

*new combination synonyms used widely in the aquarium hobby

Chaetodon aya Jordan, 1886 – W. Atlantic, Vol. 2, p. 170

Chaetodon eques Steindachner, 1903

Chaetodon dichrous Günther, 1869 – Ascension and St. Helena islands, Vol. 2, p. 180

Chaetodon falcifer Hubbs and Rechnitzer, 1958 – E. Pacific, Vol. 2, p. 182

Chaetodon guezei Maugé and Bauchot, 1976 – Réunion, Vol. 2, p. 188

Chaetodon guyanensis Durand, 1960 – W. Atlantic, Vol. 2, p. 190

Chaetodon goniodes Woods, 1961

Chaetodon marcellae Poll, 1950 – W. Africa, Vol. 2, p. 198

Chaetodon altipinnis Cadenat, 1950

Subgenus *Radophorus*

Dorsal rays XII–XIV, 20–25; anal rays III, 19–22; dorsal and anal fins with blunt angle posteriorly; snout pointed, slightly projecting, 1.9–2.8 in head length; lateral line in a high, angular arc; lacrymal free and smooth; scales angular.

Chaetodon auriga Forsskål, 1775 – Indo-West Pacific, Vol. 1, p. 15; Vol. 2, p. 167

Chaetodon setifer Bloch, 1793
Pomacantrus filamentosus Lacépède, 1802
Chaetodon sebanus Cuvier, 1831

Chaetodon decussatus Cuvier, 1831 – E. Indian Ocean, Vol. 2, p. 178

Chaetodon pictus (non Forsskål) Bleeker, 1852
Chaetodon vagabundus var. *jordani* Ahl, 1923

Chaetodon ephippium Cuvier, 1831 – Indo-West Pacific, Vol. 1, p. 21

Chaetodon principalis Cuvier, 1831
Chaetodon garnotii Lesson, 1835
Chaetodon melsanti Thiollière, 1857

Chaetodon falcula Bloch, 1793 – Indian Ocean, Vol. 2, p. 183

Chaetodon dizoster Valenciennes, 1831

Chaetodon gardineri Norman, 1939 – Gulfs of Oman and Aden, Vol. 2, p. 187

Chaetodon leucopleura Playfair, 1866 – Zanzibar to Red Sea, Vol. 2, p. 194

Chaetodon leucopygus Ahl, 1923

Chaetodon lineolatus Cuvier, 1831 – Indo-West Pacific, Vol. 1, p. 25

Chaetodon lunatus Cuvier, 1831
Chaetodon tallii Bleeker, 1854

Chaetodon mesoleucos Forsskål, 1775 – Red Sea, Vol. 2, p. 202

Chaetodon hadjan Bloch, 1801

Chaetodon nigropunctatus Sauvage, 1880 – Gulf of Oman and Persian Gulf, Vol. 2, p. 210

Chaetodon obscurus Boulenger, 1887

Chaetodon oxycephalus Bleeker, 1853 – Melanesia to Sri Lanka, Vol. 2, p. 215

Chaetodon rafflesi Bennett, 1830 – W. Pacific and E. Indian Ocean, Vol. 1, p. 38

Chaetodon princeps Cuvier, 1831
Chaetodon sebae Cuvier, 1831
Chaetodon dahli Ahl, 1923

Chaetodon selene Bleeker, 1853 – E. Indies to S. Japan, Vol. 1, p. 42

Chaetodon semeion Bleeker, 1855 – W. Pacific, Vol. 1, p. 43

Chaetodon ulietensis Cuvier, 1831 – W. Pacific, Vol. 1, p. 50

Chaetodon aurora De Vis, 1885
Chaetodon ulietensis var. *confluens* Ahl, 1923

Chaetodon vagabundus Linnaeus, 1758 – Indo-West Pacific, Vol.1, p. 52

Chaetodon pictus Forsskål, 1775
Chaetodon nesogallicus Cuvier, 1831

Chaetodon xanthocephalus Bennett, 1832 – W. Indian Ocean, Vol. 2, p. 235

Chaetodon nigripinnatus Desjardins, 1836
Chaetodon nigripinnis Peters, 1855
Chelmo pulcher Steindachner, 1875
Chaetodon auromarginatus Bliss, 1883
Chaetodon dayi Ahl, 1923

Subgenus *Rhombochaetodon*

Dorsal rays XIII, 20–23; anal rays III, 16–17; spinous dorsal rounded to nearly triangular; soft dorsal fin rounded posteriorly, anal fin angular; snout pointed, 2.6–3.2 in length of head; lateral line in a low arc; scales rhomboid, arranged in a chevron pattern.

Chaetodon argentatus Smith and Radcliffe, 1911 – E. Indies to Japan, Vol. 2, p. 166

Chaetodon madagascariensis Ahl, 1923 – Indian Ocean, Vol. 2, p. 196

Chaetodon chrysurus Desjardins, 1833

Chaetodon mertensii Cuvier, 1831 – W. Pacific, Vol. 1, p. 30

Chaetodon dixoni Regan, 1904

Chaetodon paucifasciatus Ahl, 1923 – Red Sea, Vol. 2, p. 216

Chaetodon xanthurus Bleeker, 1857 – E. Indies to Okinawa, Vol. 2, p. 236

Subgenus *Roa*

Dorsal rays XIII, 19–22; anal rays III, 16; spinous dorsal with triangular shape, 3rd or 4th spine the longest; 2nd anal spine significantly longer than 3rd; rear edge of dorsal and anal fins approximately vertical; snout pointed, 2.7–3.7 in length of head; ocular band vertical below eye; scaly sheath of dorsal fin low.

Chaetodon burgessi Allen and Starck, 1973 – Palau and Philippines, Vol. 2, p. 172

Chaetodon declivis Randall, 1975 – Marquesas Islands, Vol. 2, p. 177

Chaetodon declevis Burgess and Randall, 1978

Chaetodon mitratus Günther, 1860 – Indian Ocean, Vol. 2, p. 206

Chaetodon modestus Temminck and Schlegel, 1842 – Indo-West Pacific, Vol. 2, p. 208

Coradion desmotes Jordan and Fowler, 1902

Loa excelsa Jordan, 1922

Chaetodon jayakari Norman, 1939

*Heniochus excelsa Gosline, 1965

Chaetodon nippon Steindachner and Döderlein, 1884 – Philippines to Japan, Vol. 2, p. 211

Chaetodon carens Seale, 1910

Chaetodon decipiens Ahl, 1923

Chaetodon tinkeri Schultz, 1951 – Hawaiian Islands, Vol. 2, p. 230

Subgenus *Tetrachaetodon*

Dorsal rays XIV, 16–17; anal rays III–IV, 15–16; dorsal spines graduated; dorsal and anal fins rounded posteriorly; snout blunt and short, 3.0–4.0 in length of head; lateral line in a low arc; lacrymal partly hidden by scales; base of spinous dorsal fin about twice length of soft dorsal base; scales rounded.

Chaetodon bennetti Cuvier, 1831 – Indo-West Pacific, Vol. 1, p. 18

Chaetodon vinctus Bennett, 1839

Chaetodon plebeius Cuvier, 1831 – Indo-West Pacific, Vol. 1, p. 35

Chaetodon cordiformis Thiollière, 1856

Megaprotodon maculiceps Ogilby, 1910

Chaetodon speculum Cuvier, 1831 – W. Pacific, Vol. 1, p. 44

Chaetodon spilopleura Cuvier, 1831

Chaetodon ocellifer Franz, 1910

Chaetodon zanzibariensis Playfair, 1866 W. Indian Ocean, Vol. 2, p. 237

Genus *Chelmon* Cloquet, 1817

Dorsal spines 9; dorsal fin spines increasing in length posteriorly; lateral line complete with 45–55 scales; snout elongate, 1.7–3.0 in length of head; no scales on lacrymal bone.

Chelmon marginalis Richardson, 1842 – N. Australia, Vol. 1, p. 56

Chelmo tricinctus Castelnau, 1876

Chelmon mülleri (Klunzinger, 1879) – N. E. Australia, Vol. 1, p. 57

Chelmon rostratus (Linnaeus, 1758) – far W. Pacific and Indian Ocean, Vol. 1, p. 58

Chaetodon enceladus Shaw and Nodder, 1791

Chelmon lol Thiollière, 1857

Genus *Chelmonops* Bleeker, 1876

Dorsal spines 11; dorsal fin spines increasing in length posteriorly; lateral line complete with 51–56 scales; snout elongate, 2.2–2.6 in length of head; no scales on lacrymal bone.

Chelmonops truncatus (Kner, 1859) – S. Australia, Vol. 1, p. 60

Chelmo trochilus Günther, 1874

Genus *Coradion* Kaup, 1860

Dorsal spines 8–10; dorsal fin spines increasing in length posteriorly; lateral line complete with 43–52 scales; snout short, 2.9–3.8 in length of head; lacrymal bone scaled.

Coradion altivelis McCulloch, 1916 – Australia to Japan, Vol. 1, p. 62

Coradion fulvocinctus Tanaka, 1918

Coradion chrysozonus (Cuvier, 1831) – Australia to China, Vol. 1, p. 64

Chaetodon labiatus Cuvier, 1831

Chaetodon guttatus Gray, 1854

Coradion melanopus (Cuvier, 1831) – E. Indies to New Guinea, Vol. 1, p. 66

Genus *Forcipiger* Jordan & McGregor, 1898

Dorsal spines 11 or 12; spinous dorsal deeply incised between spines; lateral line complete with 66–80 scales; snout elongate, 1.4–2.1 in length of head; lacrymal bone partly scaled.

Forcipiger flavissimus Jordan and McGregor, 1898 – Indo-Pacific, Vol. 1, p. 68

Forcipiger longirostris (Broussonet, 1782) – Indo-Pacific, Vol. 1, p. 69; Vol. 2, p. 338

Forcipiger cyrano Randall, 1961

Forcipiger inornatus Randall, 1961

*new combination synonyms used widely in the aquarium hobby

Genus *Hemitaurichthys* Bleeker, 1876

Dorsal spines 12 to 16; dorsal fin rounded in shape; lateral line complete with 70–90 scales; snout short, 2.5–3.6 in length of head; lacrymal bone partly scaled.

Hemitaurichthys multispinosus Randall, 1975 – Pitcairn Island, Vol. 2, p. 238

> *Hemitaurichthys multispinus* Burgess and Randall, 1978

Hemitaurichthys polylepis (Bleeker, 1857) – W. Pacific, Vol. 1, p. 70

Hemitaurichthys thompsoni Fowler, 1923 – Hawaiian Islands, Vol. 2, p. 239

Hemitaurichthys zoster (Bennett, 1831) – Indian Ocean, Vol. 2, p. 240

Genus *Heniochus* Cuvier, 1817

Dorsal spines 11 or 12; 4th dorsal spine elongate; lateral line complete with 40–60 scales; snout moderate, 2.5–4.5 in head length; lacrymal bone partly scaled.

Heniochus acuminatus (Linnaeus, 1758) – Indo-West Pacific, Vol. 1, p. 73; Vol. 2, p. 341

> *Chaetodon macrolepidotus* Linnaeus, 1758
> *Chaetodon bifasciatus* Shaw, 1803
> *Chaetodon mycteryzans* Gray, 1854

Heniochus chrysostomus Cuvier, 1831 – W. Pacific, Vol. 1, p. 74

> *Heniochus melanistion* Bleeker, 1854
> *Heniochus drepanoides* Thiollière, 1857

Heniochus diphreutes Jordan, 1903 – Indo-West Pacific, Vol. 1, p. 75; Vol. 2, p. 341

Heniochus intermedius Steindachner, 1893 – Red Sea, Vol. 2, p. 242

Heniochus monoceros Cuvier, 1831 – Indo-West Pacific, Vol. 1, p. 76

> *Heniochus permutatus* Cuvier, 1831

Heniochus pleurotaenia Ahl, 1923 – E. Indian Ocean, Vol. 2, p. 244

Heniochus singularius Smith and Radcliffe, 1911 – far W. Pacific and E. Indian Ocean, Vol. 1, p. 78

Heniochus varius (Cuvier, 1829) – W. Pacific and E. Indian Ocean, Vol. 1, p. 79

> *Taurichthys viridis* Cuvier, 1829
> *Taurichthys bleekeri* Castelnau, 1875

Genus *Johnrandallia* Nalbant, 1974

Dorsal spines 12; 4th dorsal spine the longest, remaining spines decreasing in length; lateral line complete with 52–63 scales; snout short, 3.0–3.5 in length of head; no scales on lacrymal bone.

Johnrandallia nigrirostris (Gill, 1863) – E. Pacific, Vol. 2, p. 245

> *Chaetodon nigrirostris* Jordan and Gilbert, 1882
> *Heniochus nigrirostris* Hubbs and Rechnitzer, 1958
> *Pseudochaetodon nigrirostris* Burgess, 1978

Genus *Parachaetodon* Bleeker, 1874

Dorsal spines 6; dorsal spines increasing in length posteriorly; lateral line incomplete with 40–43 scales; snout short, 2.8–3.8 in length of head; lacrymal bone scaled.

Parachaetodon ocellatus (Cuvier, 1831) – far W. Pacific and E. Indian Ocean, Vol. 1, p. 82

> *Chaetodon obligacanthus* Bleeker, 1850
> *Chaetodon townleyi* De Vis, 1885

In addition to the characters mentioned above, the general body shapes or outlines of the various genera and subgenera are diagnostic.

*new combination synonyms used widely in the aquarium hobby

Genus: *Amphichaetodon*

Amphichaetodon melbae
San Felix Butterflyfish

BURGESS and CALDWELL, 1978

This species is known on the basis of 17 specimens collected at San Felix Island off the coast of Chile (approximately 27° S latitude). It is similar morphologically to *Amphichaetodon howensis* (Vol. 1, p. 59) from Lord Howe Island, New South Wales, and New Zealand, but differs primarily in color pattern. Both species possess a series of five vertical bars on the head and body, but in *melbae* these bars are relatively narrow, with much broader areas of pale color between them; in *howensis* the main dark bars are approximately equal in width or wider than the pale spaces between. The habitat consists primarily of rocky reef, but the depth distribution is poorly documented. This species is presently unknown to the aquarium trade. Captive specimens would require special cool water conditions with an optimum temperature range of approximately 16 to 19° C (61 to 66° F). The maximum size is about 16 cm (6.4 in.).

215.
Amphichaetodon melbae. Only black-and-white photos of preserved specimens were available. Therefore a drawing showing the actual colors was made for this book by Martin Thompson.

Genus: *Chaetodon*   Butterflyfishes

Chaetodon aculeatus   (POEY, 1860)
Caribbean Longsnout Butterflyfish

The Caribbean Longsnout Butterflyfish is distributed throughout the West Indian region from southern Florida to Curaçao, off the Venezuelan coast. It generally occurs on deep reefs but Dr. John Randall has observed it in as little as one meter of water along a rocky shore at Curaçao. Most collections and observations of this species have been at depths between 20 and 50 meters (66 and 160 ft). The maximum depth record is 91 meters (298 ft). The species is frequently found adjacent to steep dropoffs or on their upper edges and is sometimes seen in caves or caverns. Off southern Florida the fish is frequently seen between 20 and 30 meters (66 and 98 ft) where the habitat consists primarily of large head-forming corals, sponges, and alcyonarians. It is generally a solitary species, but sometimes moves about in pairs. The young occasionally form aggregations of eight to 10 fish. The diet apparently consists largely of small crustaceans and other invertebrates which are picked from the coral and the spines of sea urchins. This species is popular in the aquarium trade and is sometimes sold under the name "Ross Butterflyfish". It is a hardy species that is easier to keep than most butterflyfishes.

216.
Chaetodon (Progna-thodes) aculeatus
Photo of a subadult in an aquarium in Sydney.
Photo: Friese.

217.
Chaetodon aculeatus
Aquarium photo of a subadult. It rarely grows more than 10 cm (4 in.) in length.
Photo: Kahl.

216 ▲   217 ▼

Chaetodon argentatus
Asian Butterflyfish

SMITH and RADCLIFFE, 1911

The original description of this species was based on two specimens collected in 1908 and 1909 off southern Luzon in the Philippines. Since then further collecting has expanded the known distribution. It is now recorded as far north as southern Japan, Taiwan, and the Ryukyu Islands. In Japan it is said to be common from Tanabe Bay (on southern Honshu, about 450 km (281 miles) southeast of Tokyo), southward, and is also present at Hachijo Island (approximately 280 km [175 miles] due south of Tokyo). In the Japanese portion of the range it is found in rocky areas, but farther to the south it inhabits coral reefs. The species is generally encountered in pairs or small aggregations at depths between five and 20 meters (16 and 66 ft). The Asian Butterflyfish belongs to the

xanthurus species complex, a group characterized by a dark network on the sides and a band of red, orange, or brown pigmentation across the posterior-most part of the body. It is a hardy species that does well in captivity. Aquarium imports from the Philippines and Hong Kong are common. The maximum size is about 20 cm (8 in.).

218.
Chaetodon argentatus
Aquarium photo of an adult of 10 cm (4 in.) in length.
Photo:
Nieuwenhuizen.

219.
Chaetodon argentatus
Juvenile, 3.3 cm (1.3 in.). Taiwan.
Photo: Randall.

◄ 218   219 ▼

Chaetodon auriga
Threadfin Butterflyfish

FORSSKÅL, 1775

This species is included in both volumes because some authorities recognize two subspecies: *C. auriga auriga* Forsskål and *C. auriga setifer* Bloch. The latter variety is widely distributed in the tropical Indo-Pacific from Hawaii to East Africa and was featured in Volume 1. *C. auriga auriga* is confined to the Red Sea. Both forms are similar in appearance, but the adults of the Red Sea fish lack the black spot on the soft dorsal fin and generally possess a much shorter filament on the posterior part of the dorsal. This species is relatively common throughout the Red Sea and may be seen in a variety of habitats ranging from rich coral reefs to weed and rubble covered areas. It is found singly, in pairs, and in aggregations that roam over large distances in search of food, primarily corals and other small invertebrates such as crabs and shrimps. The young of this species are particularly well suited for life in captivity. A wide variety of dry and frozen fish foods are accepted, and if properly cared for, it will thrive for several years in an aquarium. The maximum size is about 18 cm (7.2 in.), but aquarium specimens seldom grow that large.

221.
Chaetodon auriga
14 cm (5.5 in.) in length. Red Sea, Jeddah, at a depth of 18 m (59 ft).
Photo: Debelius.

220.
Chaetodon auriga
Adult in night coloration. Underwater photo from the Red Sea.
Photo: Moosleitner.

▼ 220

221 ▶

Chaetodon auripes
Oriental Butterflyfish

JORDAN and SNYDER, 1901

222 ▲

223 ▼

This species is distributed from the vicinity of Tokyo, Japan south to Taiwan. According to Masuda *et al.* (1975), it is common in Japan around the southern portion of Honshu, Shikoku, and Kyushu. In these waters it is able to survive winter temperatures which sometimes drop as low as 10° C (50° F). *Chaetodon auripes* has been confused with *C. collare* by many earlier authors. The Oriental Butterflyfish is often referred to as *Chaetodon aureus* Schlegel (1844), but the specific name *aureus* is preoccupied by *Chaetodon aureus* Bloch (1787) which is a junior synonym of *Pomacanthus arcuatus,* the Grey Angelfish. Small juveniles have a black ocellus on the soft dorsal fin which gradually disappears with increasing size. They also exhibit a dark band across the base of the tail and the caudal fin is transparent. This species is relatively hardy and does well in captivity but it is seldom seen in Europe and America. The maximum size is about 20 cm (8 in.).

222.
Chaetodon auripes
Juvenile, ca. 5 cm
(2 in.). Underwater
photo, northern Tai-
wan.
Photo: Randall.

223.
Chaetodon auripes
Aquarium photo of an
adult from Taiwan.
Photo: Shen.

Chaetodon austriacus
Exquisite Butterflyfish

RÜPPELL, 1835

This beautifully marked species is found only in the Red Sea. On the basis of shape and coloration it is an obvious close relative of the widely distributed *C. trifasciatus* and *C. melapterus* of the Persian Gulf and Gulf of Oman. It is most similar to *trifasciatus,* but, unlike that species, the anal and caudal fins are dark in color. It prefers rich coral areas, usually in depths of less than 12 to 15 meters (39 to 50 ft). Solitary individuals or pairs are most often encountered, but occasionally small schools can be seen foraging over the reef. The species appears to be relatively common throughout the Red Sea, particularly in the Gulf of Aqaba (northern Red Sea), and farther to the south off Jeddah and Port Sudan. Apparently this species feeds exclusively on live corals and for this reason is extremely difficult to maintain in captivity. A few marine aquarists at Eilat on the Red Sea coast have been able to keep it alive for extended periods by placing small pieces of live coral in the tank every few days. This method, however, is obviously impractical for most hobbyists. The maximum size is approximately 13 cm (5.2 in.). Small juveniles lack the intense markings of adults but are nevertheless very attractive.

224.
Chaetodon austriacus
Juvenile, 3.5 cm (1.4 in.). Underwater photo, Jeddah, Red Sea. Unlike the adults which roam widely in search of food, juveniles spend most of the time among the branches of a single coral head.
Photo: Debelius.

225.
Chaetodon austriacus
Adult, 12.5 cm (5 in.) in length. Eilat, Red Sea, at a depth of 6 m (20 ft).
Photo: Allen.

224 ▲

225 ▼

Chaetodon aya
Doubleband Butterflyfish

JORDAN, 1866

This species belongs to a group of closely related butterflyfishes that dwell on deeper offshore reefs in the tropical eastern Pacific and Atlantic. All members of the group have a similar body shape characterized by prominent dorsal spines and similar color patterns in which black and white predominate. *C. aya* is the most broadly distributed member of the group. Its range extends along the section of the continental shelf bordering the Florida Peninsula and the Gulf of Mexico. It also ranges northward in the warm Gulf Stream to the vicinity of Cape Hatteras, North Carolina. Other members of this species group are *C. guyanensis* from the southern Caribbean, *C. marcellae* from West Africa, and *C. falcifer* from the tropical eastern Pacific. Because of its preference for deep water *C. aya* is seldom seen by divers, but it is apparently common at depths between 45 and 150 meters (148 and 490 ft) where water temperatures range from 16−22° C (60.8−71.6° F). SCUBA divers occasionally encounter it at depths as shallow as 30 meters (100 ft), but most specimens have been collected by trawlers working in deeper water. The first specimen which was the basis for the original description of *C. aya* was collected in a most unusual manner. It was regurgitated by a red snapper caught near Pensacola, Florida, during the 1880s. Because of its deep habitat, this species is usually not available to aquarists. The maximum size is about 15 cm (6 in.).

226.
Chaetodon aya
The painting shows the characteristic form and coloration of this rare deep reef species.

Chaetodon blackburnii
Blackburn's Butterflyfish

This species is easily distinguished from all other members of the genus by its 16 dorsal spines, the highest number found in any *Chaetodon*. It is distributed along the east African coast from Kenya as far south as Bashee (about 415 km [259 miles] south of Durban). It also occurs off the island of Mauritius and is probably present at Madagascar. There have been few underwater sightings of this species, consequently there is a paucity of information on its natural history. Presumably it is an inhabitant of coral reefs. Juveniles are similar in appearance to adults, but the oblique bands are not so pronounced and there is a reduction of the pale area behind the head. The maximum size is about 13 cm (5.2 in.).

227 ▲

228 ▼

227.
Chaetodon blackburnii
Subadult, 8 cm
(3 in.) in length.
Aquarium photo.
Photo:
Nieuwenhuizen.

228.
Chaetodon blackburnii
Adult, nearly 12 cm
(4.8 in.) in length.
Aquarium photo.
Photo: Kahl.

Chaetodon burgessi
Burgess' Butterflyfish

ALLEN and STARCK, 1973

In early 1972, while stationed as a marine biologist with the Trust Territory Government in the Palau Islands, I had an opportunity to make a series of deep SCUBA dives with my good friend Dr. Walter Starck. One of the most memorable of these dives took place in the Ngemelis Islands of the southern Palau group, where we found an incredibly steep submarine cliff off Bairakaseru Island. On the upper edge of the dropoff it was possible to stand in knee-deep water at low tide and in one giant step the cliff plunged precipitously for several hundred meters: the incline was perfectly vertical and in some places actually undercut. We made several dives at this fascinating location and collected many ichthyological treasures, including several species new to science. It had long been Walter's ambition and mine to discover a new species of butterflyfish, and at Bairakaseru Island we were successful at last. On the first dive we sighted a pair of unfamiliar chaetodontids swimming among black coral on the vertical wall. We knew at once they must be new. We tried unsuccessfully to secure the fish with rotenone, a commercial fish collecting preparation. Finally, on three subsequent dives, Walter managed to spear three specimens at depths between 40 and 75 meters (130 and 246 ft). We eventually named this species *Chaetodon burgessi* in honor of Dr. Warren Burgess, the author of a comprehensive monograph on the chaetodontids. During our dives we encountered about eight pairs of *C. burgessi* in areas of the steep wall covered with black coral. The species has also been collected in the Philippine Islands which lie about 800 km (500 miles) due west of Palau. Because of its deep dwelling habits, it is virtually unknown to the aquarium trade. The maximum size is about 14 cm (5.6 in.).

229.
Chaetodon burgessi
This aquarium photo
of a very rare species
shows an adult .
Photo: Lubbock.

Chaetodon capistratus
Foureye Butterflyfish

LINNAEUS, 1758

The Foureye Butterflyfish is well known to divers and aquarists in the southeastern United States. It is the most common butterflyfish in the West Indies, and occurs throughout the Caribbean Sea, the Gulf of Mexico, and along the southeast coast of the United States. The warm Gulf Stream has greatly facilitated its dispersal along the U.S. east coast and there are records of its presence as far north as Massachusetts. The distinguishing characteristic of this species is a large "false eyespot" near the base of the tail. Presumably this marking serves to confuse potential predators by misdirecting their attacks, thus allowing the butterflyfish to escape. The species is an inhabitant of shallow reefs on which it generally occurs singly or in pairs. Its principal food items are zoantharians, polychaete worms, gorgonians, and tunicates. In captivity it readily accepts a diet that includes live and frozen brine shrimp, fresh fish, and clam meat and a variety of dry commercial preparations. It is a relatively inexpensive species that is the hardiest among the butterflyfishes and is therefore an ideal selection for the beginning marine aquarist. The maximum size is about 15 cm (6 in.). but most specimens measure less than 10 cm (4 in.).

230. ▲   231. ▼

232. ▼

230.
Chaetodon capistratus
The juvenile form has two eye-spots until it reaches a length of about 3 cm (1.2 in.).
Photo: Norman.

231.
This juvenile, at a length of about 3 cm (1.2 in.), has lost the second eye-spot. It acquires adult coloration at a length of about 5 to 6 cm (2 in.).
Photo: Norman.

232.
Chaetodon capistratus
Adult 11 cm (4.4 in.).
Underwater photo from Nassau/Bahamas.
Photo: Baensch.

Chaetodon collare
Collare Butterflyfish

BLOCH, 1787

This distinctive butterflyfish occurs in the Indonesian–Philippines region and in certain areas of the Indian Ocean including India, Sri Lanka, the Maldive Islands, Pakistan, the Gulf of Oman, and the southeast coast of the Arabian Peninsula. It somewhat resembles the Reticulated Butterflyfish, *C. reticulatus,* from the western Pacific, but unlike that species it has a red tail. The pale band behind the eye is also much narrower and lacks the yellow hue characteristic of *reticulatus* (see Vol. 1, p. 40).
I observed this species at the Thousand Islands (Pulau Seribu) in the Java Sea off Jakarta in 1975. It generally appeared in pairs on the outer reef slope at depths of five to 10 meters (16 to 33 ft). Two years later I encountered it again, this time in the vicinity of

Muscat in the Gulf of Oman. It was relatively common at this locality. Many pairs and several aggregations that contained as many as 20 fish were seen. The habitat at Muscat consisted largely of rocky reef, with limited areas of coral adjacent to the shore. The species was extremely easy to approach at close range. Most specimens were found in depths between four and 15 meters (13 and 50 ft). It is commonly exported to Europe and America, but captive specimens are sometimes difficult to acclimate to aquarium conditions, particularly in regard to diet. Much of their natural food consists of coral polyps. The maximum size is about 16 cm (6.4 in.).

233.
Chaetodon collare
An adult pair. The max. length is about 16 cm (6.3 in.). Underwater photo from the Maldive Islands. Photo: Schöpfer.

234.
Chaetodon collare
Juvenile, 5 cm (2 in.). Aquarium photo. Photo: Norman.

◀ 233

234 ▼

Chaetodon collare on the Reef, Maldive Islands

235.
Chaetodon collare
A splendid school
from the Maldives.
Photo: Langhoff.

Chaetodon daedalma
Wrought Iron Butterflyfish

JORDAN and FOWLER, 1903

This distinctive species is distributed around the
Ryukyu, Bonin, and Izu islands and the main islands
of southern Japan, where it is known from Sagami
Bay (near Tokyo), southward. It is said to be rare
except on rocky reefs in certain areas of the Izu and
Bonin islands. The species is occasionally kept in
captivity by Japanese aquarists but is seldom
exported. The maximum size is about 15 cm (6 in.).

236.
Chaetodon daedalma
Aquarium photo of a
subadult 8 cm (3.2 in.)
in length. From Japan.
Photo: Yasuda.

Chaetodon declivis
Marquesan Butterflyfish

RANDALL, 1975

This recently discovered species is closely related to *C. tinkeri* of the Hawaiian Islands. It was collected and described by Dr. John E. Randall during a seven-month cruise around southeast Oceania aboard the 30-meter (100 ft) schooner *Westward.* The species is known on the basis of six specimens, all of which were collected by spear and rotenone (a commercial ichthyocide) off the north side of Hanauu Bay at Fatu Hiva in the Marquesas Islands. The fish were collected at the base of a vertical rock wall at a depth of 23 meters (75 ft) over a bottom of rock and sand. This species differs from *C. tinkeri* by having a reddish-brown rather than a black area on the posterior part of the body and dorsal fin. In addition, *declivis* has a slightly larger eye. Because of its limited distribution and deep dwelling habits, it will probably remain unknown in the aquarium trade. The maximum size is about 12 cm (4.8 in.). The Latin name *declivis,* which means "sloping", refers to the abrupt diagonal demarcation in color pattern.

237.
Chaetodon declivis
Adult, 9 cm (4 in.) in length, Fatu Hiva, Marquesas Islands.
Photo: Randall.

Chaetodon decussatus on the Reef, Sri Lanka

Chaetodon decussatus
Indian Vagabond Butterflyfish

CUVIER, 1831

The Indian Vagabond Butterflyfish is closely related to *Chaetodon vagabundus* (see Vol. 1, p. 52) but differs primarily in color pattern. On *vagabundus* the soft dorsal and anal fins are yellow with a distinct black band just forward of the yellow area; however, in *C. decussatus* the entire posterior part of the body is blackish and the yellow coloration is absent except for a narrow marginal band and a slightly wider submarginal band on the anal fin. *Chaetodon decussatus* occurs on the coral reefs of Sri Lanka, the Maldive Islands, India, Andaman Sea, and the westernmost portion of the Indo-Malayan Archipelago. *C. vagabundus,* on the other hand, is a wide-ranging species found over most of the tropical Indo-West Pacific. At Sri Lanka *C. decussatus* is one of the most common butterflyfishes and is found in many habitats ranging from rich coral reefs to rubble and rocky areas. The depth range extends from only one or two meters (3.3 to 6.6 ft) to at least 20 meters (66 ft). This species is occasionally imported from Sri Lanka and is an excellent aquarium fish once it begins feeding. In nature the diet consists largely of algae and coral polyps, but captive fish will accept a wide variety of items including dry and frozen foods. The maximum size is about 20 cm (8 in.).

238.
Chaetodon decussatus
Among aquarists this species is better known under its synonym *Chaetodon pictus.* This underwater photo shows a pair on the steep reefs near Sri Lanka at a depth of about 30 m (100 ft).
Photo: Jonklaas.

239.
Chaetodon decussatus
Subadult, 8 cm (3.2 in.). Aquarium photo.
Photo: Norman.

◄ 238

239 ▼

Chaetodon dichrous
Hedgehog Butterflyfish

GÜNTHER, 1869

This is one of the lesser known butterflyfish species. It occurs only at St. Helena and Ascension islands in the middle of the tropical Atlantic Ocean. At Ascension it is generally uncommon and primarily restricted to depths below 12 meters (39 ft). However, it can usually be seen around a 0 to 12 meter (39 ft) dropoff in the vicinity of Hummock Point. It usually occurs in pairs, which browse over the rocky substratum, presumably in search of benthic invertebrates. The white rectangular marking on the body is conspicuous when observed underwater. This species is unknown to marine aquarium enthusiasts. The maximum size is about 16 cm (6.4 in.).

240 ▲

241 ▼

240.
Chaetodon dichrous
An adult from Ascension Island in the middle of the Atlantic Ocean
Photo: Lubbock.

241.
Chaetodon dichrous
Ascension Island.
Underwater photo of an adult.
Photo: Lubbock.

Chaetodon dolosus
African Butterflyfish

AHL, 1923

The African Butterflyfish is one of the least known members of the family. Relatively few specimens have been collected and nearly all were trawled in deep (40 to 200 m / 130 to 656 ft) water. It resembles the Lemon Butterflyfish (*C. miliaris*) and some authors have considered them synonymous. It differs, however, from the members of the *miliaris* species group (i. e., *miliaris, güntheri,* and *assarius*) by its darkened posterior area, and in this respect is similar to *C. sedentarius* of the western Atlantic; it is easily distinguished from *sedentarius* by a dark spot on the soft dorsal fin. The known distribution extends from northern Natal northward to the Somali coast. This species has sometimes been called *C. mendoncae.* The maximum size is about 14 cm (5.6 in.).

242.
Chaetodon dolosus
Also known as
Chaetodon mendon-cae. Underwater
photo of a subadult
from Shimoni,
Kenya/Africa.
Photo: Lubbock.

Chaetodon falcifer
Scythe Butterflyfish

HUBBS and RECHNITZER, 1958

This distinctly marked species was first described from Guadelupe Island, off Baja California. More recently it has been taken or observed at West San Benito Island (Baja California), Albermarle Island in the Galápagos, off Cape San Lucas at the tip of Baja California, near San Diego, California, and at Santa Catalina Island, off Los Angeles. The species is known on the basis of only a few specimens, although others have been observed by Dr. Richard Rosenblatt from a Costeau diving saucer off Cape San Lucas. According to his observations *C. falcifer* was seen in rocky areas at depths between 30 and 150 meters (100 and 490 ft); the largest concentration appeared at approximately 100 meters (330 ft). The shallowest records for this species are 10 to 12 meters (33 to 39 ft) at the Galápagos and 13 meters (43 ft) at Santa Catalina Island. The water temperature at the various collecting localities ranged between 16 and 20° C (61 and 68° F). *C. falcifer* is closely related to *C. aya* and *C. guyanensis* of the tropical western Atlantic and *C. marcellae* from West Africa. These four species are typically deep dwelling fishes, frequently associated with steep submarine cliffs. They are seldom collected and are therefore rarely seen in the aquarium trade. Because of its unique color pattern, *C. falcifer* is not likely to be confused with any other species. The maximum size is about 16 cm (6.4 in.).

243.
Chaetodon falcifer
Underwater photo
from the Galápagos
Islands.
Photo: Graves.

244.
Chaetodon falcifer
The first color photo
ever made of this spe-
cies. Adult.
Photo: Powell.

◄ 243

244 ▼

Chaetodon falcula
Saddleback Butterflyfish

BLOCH, 1793

This species is closely related to *Chaetodon ulietensis* (see Vol. 1) of the western Pacific but differs primarily in coloration. Both species possess a pair of dark bars on the upper side, but in *falcula* the black pigmentation is more intense and the bars tend to be more strongly wedge shaped and do not extend as far down on the sides. *C. falcula* is restricted to the Indian Ocean, and the distribution includes the Nicobar and Andaman islands, India, Sri Lanka, the Maldive Islands, the Seychelles, Mauritius, and the east coast of Africa. It is generally seen in pairs or small aggregations that may contain as many as 20 individuals. The habitat consists of coral reefs at depths between three and 15 meters (10 and 50 ft). The species is frequently exported from Sri Lanka and small specimens do well in captivity. The maximum size is about 20 cm (8 in.).

245.
Chaetodon falcula
Adult from Mayotte, Comores, a group of islands between Madagascar and South Africa.
Photo: Roediger.

Chaetodon fasciatus
Red Sea Raccoon Butterflyfish

FORSSKÅL, 1775

This species of butterflyfish is closely related to C. lunula of the tropical Indo-Pacific, discussed in Vol. 1. It is restricted to the Red Sea and differs from lunula primarily in color pattern. It lacks the black spot at the base of the caudal fin as well as the pattern of oblique yellow stripes behind the head, features that are characteristic of lunula. In addition, the dorsal and anal fins are a much brighter yellow in fasciatus and there are fewer slanting dark stripes on the sides. Although not particularly rare, this species always attracts attention because of its beauty. This particularly photogenic fish is easily approached underwater and is most often encountered alone or in pairs in areas of rich coral growth. The depth range extends from about two meters to at least 25 meters (6 to

246.
Chaetodon fasciatus
Portrait of an adult.
Underwater photo
from the Red Sea.
Photo: Moosleitner.

247.
Chaetodon fasciatus

Juvenile, 3 cm (1.2 in.).
Underwater photo
from the Red Sea.
Photo: Debelius.

248.
Chaetodon fasciatus
Adult individual in
night coloration.
Underwater photo,

Red Sea.
Photo: Moosleitner.
249.
Chaetodon fasciatus
Adult, 17 cm (6.8 in.).
Underwater photo
from Eilat, Red Sea, at
a depth of 10 m
(33 ft).
Photo: Allen.

246 ▲   247 ▼   248 ►

Chaetodon fasciatus on the Reef, Red Sea

82 ft). It is a relatively large species that attains a maximum length of about 25 cm (10 in.). Therefore only juveniles and subadults are suited for most marine aquaria but it is a hardy species that does well in captivity. It is fond of browsing on the algae that grow on the walls of the tank and will accept a wide variety of fresh, frozen, and dried food items. In nature a significant portion of the diet is composed of coral polyps.

249 ▼

Chaetodon fremblii
Bluestripe Butterflyfish

250.
Chaetodon fremblii
Adult individual over a rocky bottom Hanauma Bay, Oahu (Hawaiian Islands). In an aquarium, this fish acts aggressively towards others of the same species.
Photo: Randall.

251.
Chaetodon fremblii
Nearly adult, 9 cm (3.5 in.). Aquarium photo.
Photo: Norman.

250 ▲   251 ▼

Chaetodon fremblii was the second most common butterflyfish on the island of Oahu, Hawaii, during a 10-month survey I made during 1967–1968. The only species that was more abundant in shallow coastal waters was *C. miliaris*. The normal depth range for the adults of *C. fremblii* extends from about four meters to at least 65 meters (13 to 213 ft). Although the Bluestripe Butterflyfish is found in a variety of habitats, it appears to be especially fond of rocky areas. It is restricted to the Hawaiian Islands, being common around the high islands to the southeast and in the Leeward group. The juveniles of this species are observed from April to September on shallow protected reef flats. They are particularly attractive and much sought after by aquarium enthusiasts. The adults are often solitary in habit but also occur in pairs and small aggregations of about three to 15 fish. It is sometimes observed feeding on the eggs of damselfishes such as *Chromis ovalis* and *Abudefduf abdominalis*. Their diet is also composed of a variety of benthic invertebrates, which includes coral polyps, worms, and small crustacea. Unfortunately it is often difficult to maintain the bright colors of this species when it is kept in captivity. Adult specimens are especially notorious in this respect and for this reason juveniles are recommended for the aquarium. The maximum size is about 13 cm (5.2 in.).

Chaetodon gardineri
Gardiner's Butterflyfish

NORMAN, 1939

In spite of its attractive appearance this species has received little publicity, probably because of its limited distribution and relatively deep dwelling habits. Its geographic range extends from Sri Lanka westward to the southeastern coast of the Arabian Peninsula, or roughly the area known as the Arabian Sea in the northwestern corner of the Indian Ocean. Before the widespread use of SCUBA equipment few specimens were known. Most of the recent sightings have been in Sri Lanka at depths below 25 meters (82 ft). During 1977 I was surprised to find specimens offered for sale at the local fish market in Mutrah, near Muscat on the Gulf of Oman. Evidently they were captured with gill nets or deep traps, both methods commonly used by Arab fishermen. Despite numerous dives on coastal reefs at the northeastern tip of the Arabian Peninsula between Muscat and Khor Fakkan (United Arab Emirates), this butterflyfish was seen on only one occasion. A small group was sighted at the base of a rocky cliff at a depth of 28 meters (92 ft) on a small offshore island several kilometers north of Muscat. The species is rarely obtainable in captivity, although it is occasionally exported from Sri Lanka. The maximum size is approximately 17 cm (6.8 in.).

252.
Chaetodon gardineri
Adult. Underwater photo from Sri Lanka, at a depth of 15 m (50 ft).
Photo: Jonklaas.

253.
Chaetodon gardineri
Aquarium photo of an adult from Sri Lanka.
Photo: Lubbock.

252 ▲

253 ▼

Chaetodon guezei
Guezei's Butterflyfish

MAUGÉ and BAUCHOT, 1976

This most recently discovered member of the butterflyfish family was collected for the first time in 1973 and 1974. It is known only on the basis of two specimens, both of which were taken with a set-net at a depth of 80 meters (260 ft) in the Bay of Saint Paul on the island of Réunion in the western Indian Ocean. The painting presented here represents the first color illustration of this species. It was prepared from color notes and a black and white drawing included in the original published description. The

species is easily distinguished from other butterfly-fishes in the western Indian Ocean by its long snout. The only other chaetodontid with a longer snout in the area is the easily recognizable *Forcipiger flavissimus.* No specimens have ever been taken alive. Consequently there are no aquarium data for this species. The maximum size is about 11 cm (4.4 in.).

254.
Chaetodon guezei
This long-snouted species was discovered in 1973. Unfortunately, no photos of live or fresh specimens were taken. Therefore a painting of this species was made by Martin Thompson.

Chaetodon guttatissimus   BENNETT, 1832
Spotted Butterflyfish

The Spotted Butterflyfish is a member of a species complex that also contains *C. multicinctus, C. punctatofasciatus,* and *C. pelewensis.* The overall appearance is most similar to *C. punctatofasciatus* which was featured in Vol. 1. However, it lacks the pronounced vertical bands of that species and its eye band is solid black and uninterrupted; in *punctatofasciatus* this band is broken on the forehead and is largely orange colored. Although *C. punctatofasciatus* is primarily an inhabitant of the tropical western Pacific, *C. guttatissimus* is restricted to the Indian Ocean. Its range extends from tiny Christmas Island (about 300 km/ 188 miles due south of Java) westward to the east African coast, where it ranges as far south as Durban. It is normally an inhabitant of coral reefs and occurs singly, in pairs, or small aggregations. The principal food items for this species consist of polychaete worms, algae, and coral polyps. Aquarium specimens may prove difficult to keep alive for they are frequently reluctant to accept standard food items. Only juveniles and small sub-adults, which are more inclined to feed, are recommended. The maximum size is about 12 cm (4.8 in.).

255 ▲   256 ▼

255.
Chaetodon guttatissimus
Adult. Underwater photo from Sri Lanka, at a depth of 20 m (66 ft).
Photo: Jonklaas.

256.
Chaetodon guttatissimus
Adult, 12 cm (4.8 in.).
Aquarium photo.
Photo: Kahl.

Chaetodon guyanensis
Threeband Butterflyfish

DURAND, 1960

Chaetodon guyanensis, a close relative of *C. aya,* exhibits a similar shape and color pattern to that species. Both are inhabitants of deep reefs in the Caribbean region, but they appear to have non-overlapping distributions. *C. aya* is a resident of deep offshore reefs along the continental margin of the Gulf of Mexico and southeastern United States. *C. guyanensis* is presently known on the basis of only a few specimens collected off Puerto Rico, Barbados, and northern South America at depths between 100 and 200 meters (320 and 656 ft). It is a poorly known species that to my knowledge has rarely been captured alive. I am indebted to Dr. Patrick Colin of the University of Puerto Rico, for providing an 8-mm-film clip of this species taken from a deep diving research submarine. A color print was made from a single frame of the movie film, and although the image of the fish was not sharp it nevertheless served as the basis for the painting of this species by Martin Thompson. The maximum size is about 12 cm (4.8 in.).

257.
Chaetodon guyanensis
This species looks very much like *C. aya.* Because of the extreme depths in which it occurs, it rarely reaches home aquaria, though it is not a delicate species to keep in captivity provided it is carefully acclimated to shallow water.
Drawing: Thompson.

Chaetodon hoefleri
Hoefler's Butterflyfish

STEINDACHNER, 1883

This species is similar in appearance to *C. marleyi* of South Africa. It differs by having slightly lower counts for the soft dorsal and anal fins (D.22–23, A.16–17, compared with D.23–24, A.18–19 for *marleyi*). In addition, the juvenile stage of *marleyi* has a prominent spot on the dorsal fin that is lacking in *hoefleri* of a similar size. It occurs along the tropical coast of West Africa from the vicinity of Mauritania southward to Angola. Most of the sightings and collections were made in the northern Gulf of Guinea and the African coast immediately north of the Gulf as far as Dakar. Few recorded observations have been made of this species in its natural habitat. Mr. Roger Lubbock of Cambridge University (England) reports that apparently it is rare off Ghana, where he found only a single pair on a recent diving trip. The fish were sighted at a depth of 10 to 20 meters (33 to 66 ft) around an oil rig approximately 8 km (5 miles) offshore. The maximum size is about 20 cm (8 in.).

258.
Chaetodon hoefleri
Nearly adult. Underwater photo from the coast of Ghana at a depth of 20 m (66 ft).
Photo: Lubbock.

Chaetodon humeralis
East Pacific Butterflyfish

GÜNTHER, 1860

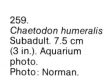

259.
Chaetodon humeralis
Subadult. 7.5 cm
(3 in.). Aquarium
photo.
Photo: Norman.

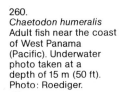

260.
Chaetodon humeralis
Adult fish near the coast
of West Panama
(Pacific). Underwater
photo taken at a
depth of 15 m (50 ft).
Photo: Roediger.

Chaetodon humeralis is broadly distributed along the eastern Pacific coast from the Gulf of California to Panama. It is by far the most common butterflyfish in the shallow waters of this region. Günther originally described it from the Sandwich (Hawaiian) Islands, but this locality is obviously an error. In early 1976 I observed this species in the Gulf of Panama in the vicinity of the Perlas Islands. It was usually sighted in pairs or small groups in rocky areas near shore at depths between two and 10 meters (6.6 and 33 ft). Individuals were easily approached at close range. Water temperatures were cool, in the vicinity of 18 to 19° C (64 to 66° F), due to the influence of deep sea upwelling. Because of the comparatively impoverished fish fauna in the eastern Pacific, there is little commercial interest in this area and consequently species such as *C. humeralis* are seldom available to marine hobbyists. Juveniles possess an ocellated spot on the soft dorsal fin and are particularly attractive. In many respects this species resembles *Chaetodon striatus* from the western Atlantic. The alternating pattern of black bands is similar but the white area between the two body bands is much broader in *humeralis*. The maximum size for this species is about 18 cm (7.2 in.).

259 ▲   260 ▼

Chaetodon larvatus CUVIER, 1831
Orange-Face Butterflyfish

This is one of the most beautifully marked species in the Red Sea. It is always associated with areas of rich coral growth at depths between three and 12 meters (10 and 39 ft). It is particularly abundant in the central Red Sea in the vicinity of Jeddah on the Arabian side and off Port Sudan on the African coast. The species is closely related to *C. baronessa* of the western Pacific (see Vol. 1) and *C. triangulum* from the Indian Ocean but differs appreciably on the basis of color pattern. Many authors have placed these species in the genus *Gonochaetodon*, thus distinguishing them from *Chaetodon* on the basis of their rhombic scale shape and unusual pattern of scalation. In addition, the body is strongly compressed and elevated and has a characteristic △ shape. Recent studies by Dr. Warren E. Burgess indicate, however, that these differences warrant subgeneric distinction only and therefore the three species should be placed in the genus *Chaetodon. C. larvatus* is usually seen in pairs, frequently in association with platelike heads of *Acropora* coral. It is a territorial species that actively chases away other butterflyfishes when they intrude into its feeding area. Their diet consists almost exclusively of coral polyps and therefore the task of maintaining this species in captivity is a difficult one. The maximum size is about 12 cm (4.8 in.). The "variety" *C. karraf* (Cuvier and Valenciennes) with a dark eye-band has never appeared again after its first description. It may represent a hybrid between *C. triangulum* and *C. larvatus.*

261.
Chaetodon larvatus
Underwater photo of an adult pair in the Red Sea.
Photo: Schuch.

Chaetodon leucopleura
Somali Butterflyfish

PLAYFAIR, 1866

This species is known from relatively few locations in the western Indian Ocean. It has been reported at several localities on the East African coast from Zanzibar northward to the Aldabra Islands, the Seychelles, and the Farsan Archipelago of the southern Red Sea. Apparently it prefers deeper water; most of the known specimens have been taken between 40 and 75 meters (130 and 246 ft). This species is most closely related to *C. gardineri* and *C. selene.* There are few records of aquarium imports, but the species appears to be relatively hardy in captivity. The maximum size is about 18 cm (7.2 in.).

262.
Chaetodon leucopleura
Aquarium photo of an adult. The species is easy to keep in captivity.
Photo: Friese.

Chaetodon litus
Easter Island Butterflyfish

RANDALL and CALDWELL, 1973

Although this species is certainly one of the most drably colored butterflyfishes, it is nevertheless an interesting one, particularly from the standpoint of its extremely limited distribution. It is known only around tiny Easter Island, that isolated rampart of volcanic rock that lies approximately 3500 km (2187 miles) west of Chile and is best known for its gigantic stone carvings. The species was taken first in 1958 by crew members of the yacht *Chiriqui* who were collecting fishes for the Los Angeles County Museum in California. Subsequent specimens were procured by members of the Canadian Medical Expedition to Easter Island in 1964 and 1965. During February 1969 I had the opportunity to make collections at Easter Island with Dr. John E. Randall on an expedition sponsored by the National Geographic Society. We obtained approximately 20 more specimens and the species was eventually described by Dr. Randall and Dr. David Caldwell. The fish fauna of Easter Island is greatly impoverished primarily because of its great isolation and subtropical position. The only other butterflyfish sighted there was the Longnose (*Forcipiger flavissimus*). The undersea habitat at Easter Island consisted largely of volcanic boulders, which frequently had a heavy covering of brown algae (*Sargassum* and *Zonaria*). Water temperatures ranged from 21–22° C (70–72° F). One or two species of coral were present, but not in great quantity, although nearly 50% of the bottom in some of the larger tidal pools consisted of live coral. We encountered specimens of *C. litus* at depths ranging from one to 25 meters (3.3 to 82 ft). The juveniles, which are somewhat paler and slightly silvery, were collected from shallow tide pools. On one occasion I observed this species "picking" at the bodies of other fishes, apparently in search of parasites. This type of cleaning behavior is well documented in the wrasse genus *Labroides* and is also exhibited by the juveniles of other wrasses and some butterflyfishes. *C. litus* obtains a maximum size of about 15 cm (6 in.).

263. ▲   264. ▼

263.
Chaetodon litus
Juvenile 3.6 cm
(1.4 in.) in length. This
photo was taken of a
specimen from
Easter Island in the
southeast Pacific.
Photo: Randall.

264.
Chaetodon litus
Adult 11.5 cm (4.6 in.).
Easter Island.
Photo: Randall.

Chaetodon madagascariensis
Madagascar Butterflyfish

AHL, 1923

This species has been referred to as *C. chrysurus* by most authors, but Burgess (1978) has shown that this name is preoccupied. It was first used by Schneider to describe a species of pomacanthid which was incorrectly placed in the genus *Chaetodon*. Therefore the next available name for this wide-ranging Indian Ocean species is *C. madagascariensis.* This species has been recorded from the East African coast, Madagascar, Mauritius, Sri Lanka, and the Cocos-Keeling Islands and recently by the author at Christmas Island, where only one individual was observed at a depth of 16 to 18 meters (52 to 59 ft) adjacent to the steep outer reef slope in an area in which the bottom was composed mainly of rubble. The color differences between *C. madagascariensis*

and *C. mertensii* are not impressive and, although Burgess (1978) recognizes two species, there is a distinct possibility that *madagascariensis* is only a subspecies or variety of *mertensii.* There is little aquarium data for this fish, but, judging from closely related species such as *C. mertensii* and *C. xanthurus*, it is probably well suited to life in captivity. The maximum size is about 14 cm (5.6 in.).

265.
Chaetodon madagascariensis
Adult 10 cm (4 in.).
Christmas Island, Indian Ocean, south of Java, at a depth of 18 m (59 ft).
Photo: Allen.

For Comparison:
C. mertensii, C. paucifasciatus, C. xanthurus

266.
*Chaetodon
paucifasciatus*
This photo from Vol. 1
is shown again for
comparison.
Photo: Norman.

267.
Chaetodon xanthurus
See also page 236.
Photo: Baensch.

268.
Chaetodon mertensii
Adult from the Mars-
hall Islands in the
Pacific Ocean. Under-
water photo at a
depth of 20 m
(66 ft).
Photo: Pat Bartlett.

266 ▲   268 ▼   267 ▲

Chaetodon marcellae
Marcella Butterflyfish

POLL, 1950

269.
Chaetodon marcellae
Aquarium photo of an adult individual from the Ghana coast, West Africa.
Photo: Lubbock.

270.
Chaetodon marcellae
A pair in typical underwater landscape at the Cape Verde Islands. Underwater photo at a depth of 15 m (50 ft).
Photo: Debelius.

269 ▲   270 ▼

The Marcella Butterflyfish is closely related to *C. aya* and *C. guyanensis* from the western Atlantic. It is widespread along the coast of tropical West Africa and, like its relatives, inhabits deep water. The range extends from Senegal as far south as the vicinity of the Congo River. It also occurs at the Cape Verde Islands and probably inhabits the offshore islands in the Gulf of Guinea. It is seldom seen by divers; virtually all the specimens collected were taken by trawl net at depths ranging between 35 and 95 meters (115 and 311 ft). The temperatures at these depths generally vary between 16 and 19° C (60 and 66° F).*C. marcellae* is unknown in the aquarium trade. The maximum size is about 14 cm (5.6 in.).

Chaetodon marleyi
South African Butterflyfish

REGAN, 1921

Chaetodon marleyi is known only from the southern tip of Africa. Unlike most members of the family it is a subtropical species. The range extends along most of the South African coastline from Lambert's Bay, situated on the Atlantic side of the Cape of Good Hope, to Delagoa Bay just north of the South Africa-Mozambique border. It is the only butterflyfish species that occurs in both the Atlantic and Pacific oceans. Its variable habitat includes rock and coral reefs and estuaries, where it lives among weeds. It has also been taken as deep as 120 meters (393 ft). Although well known among South African aquarists, this beautiful species is seldom exported. If maintained in a aquarium, it should be kept at cooler temperatures than are generally indicated for butterflyfishes; between 18 and 20° C (64 and 68° F) is recommended. The maximum size is about 18 cm (7.2 in.).

M. J. Penrith, a South African scientist, has recently published evidence showing that *C. hoefleri* of the West African coast is identical to *C. marleyi*. This information was received after this book had gone to press.

271.
Chaetodon marleyi
10 cm (4 in.) TL.
Underwater photo taken at Sodwana Bay, South Africa, at a depth of 2 m (6.6 ft).
Photo: Allen.
Compare with *C. hoefleri*, p. 191.

Chaetodon melapterus
Arabian Butterflyfish

GUICHENOT, 1862

272 ▲

273 ▼

This attractive species is closely related to *C. trifasciatus* of the Indo-West Pacific and *C. austriacus* from the Red Sea. It differs primarily in coloration and is most similar to *austriacus*, but lacks the oblong dark streak (expansion of one of the stripes) posteriorly on the upper sides, and the dorsal fin and the posterior body region are broadly black. *C. melapterus* is known mainly from the Persian Gulf, Gulf of Oman, and along the southeastern coast of the Arabian Peninsula, but it has also been recorded at the Seychelles and the island of Réunion. I have observed it underwater off Bahrain Island and near Doha, Qatar, in the Persian Gulf. Although there are rich coral reefs in these areas, the fish fauna is greatly impoverished and few specimens of *C. melapterus* were seen. It was far more common on the shallow coastal reefs off Khor Fakkan (United Arab Emirates) and Muscat (Oman), both situated in the Gulf of Oman. Aggregations of more than 20 fish were sometimes sighted near Muscat. To my knowledge this species has not been exported for the aquarium trade. Although it is an extremely handsome fish, it is primarily a live coral feeder and therefore not suited for aquarium life. The maximum size is about 12 cm (4.8 in.). Juveniles are characterized by a pale spinous dorsal fin which gradually darkens with age.

272.
Chaetodon melapterus
Juvenile 3 cm (1.2 in.).
Aquarium photo.
Photo: Norman.

273.
Chaetodon melapterus
Subadult, about 8 cm
(3 in.) in length.
Underwater photo
from Doha, Qatar, Per-
sian Gulf.
Photo: Allen.

274.
Chaetodon melapterus
Also known under the
name
Chaetodon arabicus.
Adult, 10 cm
(4 in.) in length.
Underwater photo
from Muscat, Oman
(Persian Gulf), at a
depth of 4 m (13 ft).
Photo: Allen.

274 ▼

Chaetodon mesoleucos
White-Face Butterflyfish

FORSSKÅL, 1775

275 ▲   276 ▼

This is one of several butterfly-fishes found only in the Red Sea. It does not appear to be particularly abundant; for example, I did not encounter it at Eilat in the northern part of the sea in 1975 and only a few pairs were sighted in the vicinity of Jeddah during a trip there in 1977. I found it to be a shy fish and relatively difficult to approach underwater with a camera. It was found on coral reefs at depths ranging between five and 20 meters (16 and 66 ft). This species has distinctive markings and is not likely to be confused with any other butterflyfish. It is infrequently exported and avoided by most hobbyists because of its belligerent attitude towards other tank mates. It is a hardy species if properly cared for. The maximum size is about 16 cm (6.4 in.).

275.
*Chaetodon
mesoleucos*
Adult 12.5 cm (5 in.).
Underwater photo,
Jeddah, Saudi Arabia,
Red Sea.
Photo: Allen.

276.
*Chaetodon
mesoleucos*
An aquarium photo of
this beautiful, but un-
fortunately very quar-
relsome species.
Photo:
Nieuwenhuizen.

277.
*Chaetodon
mesoleucos*
Adult pair. Under-
water photo near a
wreck in the Red Sea.
Photo: Moosleitner.

Chaetodon mesoleucos Near a Wreck in the Red Sea

Chaetodon miliaris
Lemon Butterflyfish

QUOY and GAIMARD, 1824

278.
Chaetodon miliaris
Aquarium photo of an adult from Hawaii. 12.5 cm in length (5 in.). The yellow coloration of this species fades in some individuals when kept in aquaria. Photo: Norman.

279.
Chaetodon miliaris
A school feeding on the eggs of damselfishes. *C. miliaris* is considered one of the hardiest species for a salt-water aquarium. Photo: Roediger.

278 ▲

279 ▼

This species has been reported from many scattered localities throughout the tropical Indo-Pacific. Most of these records, however, are erroneous and refer to species such as *C. güntheri,* *C. assarius,* and *C. citrinellus* which are similar in appearance. The true *miliaris* is confined to the Hawaiian Islands, where it is perhaps the most common species of butterfly-fish. It is particularly abundant in the shallow waters of the Leeward Hawaiian Islands and is also common around the main islands at the southeastern end of the chain, although fewer are seen around the island of Hawaii. The species exhibits a remarkably broad depth distribution, occurring on shallow reef flats in less than one meter and at depths greater than 250 meters (820 ft), where it has been observed by research scientists aboard submersible vessels. It occurs singly, in pairs, and frequently in huge aggregations that roam over the bottom or form midwater feeding schools. Plankton is an important part of the diet, but benthic invertebrates are also eaten. In addition, *C. miliaris* is a voracious eater of damselfish eggs and is frequently seen raiding the nests of *Chromis ovalis, Abudefduf abdominalis,* and *Dascyllus albisella.* They render themselves more or less immune to the futile attacks of the nest-guarding males of these damselfishes by virtue of their large swarming numbers. *C. miliaris* grows to a maximum size of 13 cm (5.2 in.). and is quite easy to care for under aquarium conditions. This species has a pronounced breed-

Chaetodon miliaris and Other Butterflyfishes Feeding on Fish Eggs in a Cave (Hawaiian Islands)

ing season and the small young
generally appear inshore from April
to June.

280.
Different butterfly-
fishes feeding on eggs
of *Abudefduf abdomi-
nalis.* On the right
Chaetodon lunula,
in the middle *Chaeto-
don miliaris,* and half
hidden *Chaetodon
auriga.*
Photo: Roediger.

Chaetodon mitratus
Indian Butterflyfish

GÜNTHER, 1860

281 ▲

281.
Chaetodon mitratus
From the Cocos-
Keeling Islands, south
of Sumatra.
Photo: Smith-Vaniz
and Colin.

282.
Chaetodon mitratus
Adult at Christmas
Island, south of Java.
Underwater photo, at
a depth of 50 m
(160 ft).
Photo: Allen.

282 ▼

Until 1973 this vividly marked species was known only on the basis of the holotype, the specimen on which Günther's original description was based and which is deposited at the British Museum. Although it is only a stuffed skin the characteristic color pattern is evident. It served as the sole evidence of the existence of this species for 113 years until additional specimens were reported by P. Gueze and L. A. Maugé on the island of Réunion. Others were collected one year later by William Smith-Vaniz and Patrick Colin during an American expedition to Cocos-Keeling Atoll in the eastern Indian Ocean. They encountered the species at depths below 30 meters (100 ft) adjacent to steep outer reef dropoffs. It has also been collected by Dr. John E. Randall at Mauritius in the western Indian Ocean, the source of Günther's original specimen. In addition, individuals have been sighted in the Amirante Islands and the Cosmoledo group just north of Madagascar. It was also collected and photographed underwater for the first time at Christmas Island by Roger Steene and the author in May–June 1978. Approximately 1 to 5 individuals were observed on each dive below 50 meters (160 ft) depth at this locality; 68 meters (223 ft) was the deepest record. They were confined to the steep outer-reef slope in rubble areas or among growths of black coral and sea fans. Several solitary individuals were encountered, but it was also seen in pairs and trios.
C. mitratus is similar in appearance

Portrait of *Chaetodon mitratus*

to *C. burgessi* and both belong to a complex (subgenus *Roa*) of deep dwelling butterflyfishes which also contains *C. tinkeri* from Hawaii and *C. declivis* from the Marquesas Islands. All have a characteristic body shape with pronounced dorsal spines. The third and fourth dorsal spines are typically the longest and the posterior part of the fin is shortened. Highly contrasting patterns of black and white are also typical of this group. As already mentioned, the color pattern of *C. mitratus* is similar to that of *C. burgessi,* but differs in having the black area on the posterior portion of the body covering the entire dorsal fin except the first few spines. In addition, the black bar that extends down from the nape is shorter on *burgessi* and is set in a more vertical position. Although *C. mitratus* is probably widely distributed around the islands of the tropical Indian Ocean, there is little chance of its introduction to the aquarium trade because of its deep dwelling habits. The maximum size is about 14 cm (5.6 in).

283.
An underwater portrait of *Chaetodon mitratus,* taken at a depth of 50 m (160 ft) at Christmas Island. The fish has a length of 9 cm (3.5 in.).
Photo: Allen.

Chaetodon modestus
Brown-Banded Butterflyfish

TEMMINCK and SCHLEGEL, 1842

This species appears to be widely distributed in the tropical Indo-West Pacific from the Hawaiian Islands to the southern Arabian peninsula. It is known in relatively few localities but is a deep water species throughout most of its range and therefore seldom collected. Burgess (1978) recognized three distinct species: *C. jayakari* Norman from the Arabian Sea, *C. modestus* from the far western Pacific (southern Japan to West Australia), and *C. excelsa* from the Hawaiian Islands and Guam. The differences between these three "species" are minor, however. Burgess noted only slight discrepencies in the depth of the tail base and the shape of the dorsal fin spot (round in *jayakari* and slightly ovate in the other two forms). I do not regard these differences as sufficient to merit specific recognition and prefer to unite these forms under the oldest name which is *modestus*. The first Hawaiian specimen was brought to the surface dead by the lava flow of Mauna Kea on the island of Hawaii in 1919. It was described by Jordan as a distinct genus and species, *Loa excelsa*. A second specimen was taken by the author from a midwater trawl net, during fishing operations aboard a U. S. government research vessel well offshore near the island of Oahu. Additional specimens were observed by Dr. Thomas Clarke aboard a deep diving submersible off Oahu at depths ranging between 120 and 190 meters (393 and 623 ft). He also succeeded in collecting a pair of adult specimens with deeply set gill nets. This species has possibly arrived in Hawaii from Japan by larval transport via the warm extension of the Kuroshio Current, which swings eastward from the Japanese coast in the general direction of the Hawaiian chain. The species is apparently restricted to deep water, usually in rocky areas. No aquarium data are available for this species. The maximum size is about 17 cm (6.8 in.).

284.
Chaetodon modestus
An adult 11.2 cm (4.5 in.) TL. The photo was taken near Oahu, Hawaiian Islands. This species also occurs near the coast of Western Australia at great depths and other Indian Ocean localities.
Photo: Randall.

Chaetodon multicinctus
Multiband Butterflyfish

GARRETT, 1863

This species is closely related to *C. punctatofasciatus* of the tropical western Pacific. Its distribution is restricted to the Hawaiian Islands and nearby Johnston Atoll. Around the island of Oahu it is the fourth most common butterflyfish, surpassed in abundance only by *C. miliaris, Heniochus diphreutes,* and *Chaetodon fremblii.* The species is frequently found in pairs or small aggregations at depths of five to 30 meters (16 to 100 ft). It appears to be most abundant in some sections of the Kona coast on the island of Hawaii and is frequently seen in areas in which growths of *Porites* and *Pocillopora* corals predominate. Stomach content analysis reveals that it feeds on the polyps of these corals as well as on algae, polychaete worms, and small shrimps. The young are present around the island of Oahu between April and September. Their coloration is similar to that of the adults and they make fine aquarium specimens. The maximum size is about 12 cm (4.8 in.).

285.
Chaetodon multicinctus
Adult. Aquarium photo.
Photo: Kahl.

286.
Chaetodon multicinctus
Pair. Underwater photo from the Hawaiian Islands, at a depth of 25 m (82 ft).
Photo: Roediger.

285 ▲

286 ▼

Chaetodon nigropunctatus
Black-Spotted Butterflyfish

SAUVAGE, 1880

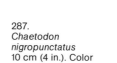

287.
Chaetodon nigropunctatus
10 cm (4 in.). Color variation from Bahrain, Persian Gulf.
Photo: Allen.

288.
Chaetodon nigropunctatus
Underwater photo from Muscat, Oman, at a depth of 6 m (20 ft).
Photo: Allen.

287 ▲

288 ▼

This is one of the less colorful members of the family. It bears a slight resemblance to *C. litus* from Easter Island but has a whitish face and slanting rows of small black spots on the sides. The geographic distribution includes the Persian Gulf, Gulf of Oman, the southeastern coast of the Arabian Peninsula, and the tropical coast of East Africa. In early 1977 I had the opportunity to observe this species in its native habitat off Bahrain and Qatar in the Persian Gulf and in the Gulf of Oman near Muscat and Khor Fakkan. It was always associated with coral reefs at depths of three to 15 meters (10 to 50 ft). Specimens from the Persian Gulf were slightly darker than those from the Gulf of Oman, which were frequently suffused with a yellowish hue, particularly towards the outer edge of the dorsal fin. The species was usually encountered singly or in pairs and was easily approached at close range. Individuals roam widely over the reef during foraging activities. Coral polyps provide at least part of their nourishment. Aquarium exports of this species are unknown. The maximum size is about 13 cm (5.2 in.).

Chaetodon nippon
Japanese Butterflyfish

STEINDACHNER and DÖDERLEIN, 1884

This species is relatively common around the islands of southern Japan. It is also known from the Philippine Islands where it was described as a separate species, *C. carens,* by Seale on the basis of an 11 cm specimen collected at Bantayan Island. In 1976 I observed and photographed this species at Miyake-jima, a beautiful volcanic island situated approximately 150 km (94 miles) south of Tokyo in the Izu Islands. A number of individuals were sighted on the rocky reefs surrounding Miyake at depths of about five to 20 meters (16 to 66 ft). The water temperature was about 20° C, (68° F), unusually warm for February, when sea temperatures of 16° C (61° F) or less are not uncommon. This is a relatively hardy species that does well in captivity. Juveniles tend to be more attractive than adults, because their yellow coloration is brighter and they also posses an ocellated spot on the soft dorsal fin. This species is not widely exported and therefore is seldom seen in captivity outside Japan. The maximum size is about 15 cm (6 in.).

289.
Chaetodon nippon
12.5 cm (5 in.). Underwater photo from Miyake-Jima, Japan, at a depth of 10 m (33 ft).
Photo: Allen.

290.
Chaetodon nippon
Juvenile, 4 cm (1.6 in) in length. Aquarium photo from Japan.
Photo: Yasuda.

291.
Chaetodon nippon
Nearly adult, 10 cm (4 in.) in length. Aquarium photo.
Photo: Norman.

◄ 289

290 ▲

291 ▼

Chaetodon ocellatus
Spotfin Butterflyfish

LINNAEUS, 1758

Although not particularly colorful compared with other members of the family, the Spotfin Butterflyfish is popular with aquarists because of its hardiness and availability. It is an inhabitant of western Atlantic coral reefs from Brazil to Florida. Larvae of this species are sometimes swept northward by the warm Gulf Stream which accounts for the sighting of juvenile specimens as far north as Massachusetts during the summer months. There is even a single record of a 3 cm (1.2 in.) specimen from Musquodoboit Harbor, Nova Scotia! The species appears to be most common on shallow Florida reefs, with fewer numbers reported around the islands of the Caribbean. The characteristic dorsal fin spot is frequently faded and therefore inconspicuous in large adults.

Small juveniles have a narrow black bar running from the dorsal spot to the anal fin, just in front of the tail base. The maximum size is about 16 cm (6.4 in.).

292.
Chaetodon ocellatus
Juvenile. 2.5 cm (1 in.) in length. Aquarium photo.
Photo: Norman.

293.
Chaetodon ocellatus
Juvenile. 5 cm (2 in.) in length. Aquarium photo.
Photo: Norman.

294.
Chaetodon ocellatus
Adult. Underwater photo taken at New Providence, Bahamas.
Photo: Roediger.

292 ▲   293 ▼   294 ▶

Juveniles of *Chaetodon ocellatus*, Swept by the Gulf Stream as Far North as New York

295 ▲   296 ▼

295/296.
Chaetodon ocellatus
Juveniles that were
driven by the Gulf
Stream to the coast of
New York. Thousands
of these fish probably
perish in November
when the waters get
colder. The butterfly-
fishes spawn on coral
reefs. Larvae and
eggs are carried
northward with the
Gulf Stream. The juve-
niles grow to a length
of up to 4–5 cm
(2 in.) before the win-
ter kill. Both photos
are rare because they
show this species in
an unusual habitat
with cold-water *Aste-
roidea* and mussels.
Adults are never
found this far north
because they can't
survive the winter.
Photos: Norman.

Chaetodon ocellicaudus
Spot-Tail Butterflyfish

CUVIER, 1831

297.
Chaetodon ocellicaudus
Juvenile, 5 cm (2 in.).
Aquarium photo.
Photo: Norman.

298.
Chaetodon ocellicaudus
Nearly adult, 9.5 cm (3.8 in.) in length.
Mactan Island, Cebu, Philippines
Photo: Randall.

297 ▲   298 ▼

This is a poorly known species, once confused with *C. melannotus* (Vol. 1, p. 28), which it greatly resembles. However, there are differences in color pattern and pectoral fin ray counts. *C. ocellicaudus* usually has 13 pectoral rays, compared with 14 rays in *C. melannotus*. The best character for distinguishing the two species is the marking at the base of the caudal fin: *C. ocellicaudus* has a pale edged, rounded black spot, whereas *C. melannotus* has an irregular black bar, which is actually an extension of the dark area on the upper back. In addition, *melannotus* has a blackish spot on the chest, which is an extension of the bar crossing through the eye; in *C. ocellicaudus* the chest marking is absent. An apparent overlap occurs in the geographic distributions of the two species, although there is no definite proof that they occur together in the same localities. *C. melannotus* is widely distributed in the Western Pacific and Indian Ocean, whereas *C. ocellicaudus* has been reported reliably only in the region extending from Timor to New Ireland (Bismarck Archipelago). Burgess (1978) states that it also ranges to the Philippines and into the Indian Ocean to Zanzibar but fails to give the source of these records. The maximum size is about 14 cm (5.6 in.).

Chaetodon oxycephalus
Spot-Nape Butterflyfish

BLEEKER, 1853

This species is similar in appearance to *C. lineolatus,* its closest relative. It differs, however, by often having fewer soft dorsal, soft anal, and pectoral *rays* (D.23–24, A. 19, P. 15, compared with the usual counts for *lineolatus:* D. 25–27, A. 20–22, P. 16). The best means of separation is color. *Chaetodon oxyce-phalus* has the same basic pattern as *lineolatus* with two notable exceptions: an interruption in the eye bar results in an isolated black spot on the nape, and the black area along the upper edge of the back extends only to the caudal fin base instead of to the middle of the anal fin base as in *lineolatus.* Burgess (1978) reported this species from the East Indies, the Philippines, Palau, New Guinea, and the eastern Indian Ocean to Sri Lanka. It is not known for certain

if it co-occurs with *C. lineolatus,* although the two species appear to have partly overlapping distribu-tions. The maximum size is about 25 cm (10 in.). *C.oxycephalus* is easy to keep in an aquarium, but is only recommended for a large tank because of the large size attained.

299.
Chaetodon oxycephalus
Adult, nearly 18 cm (7 in.) in length.
Photo: Power.

Chaetodon paucifasciatus
Red-Back Butterflyfish

AHL, 1923

300.
Chaetodon paucifasciatus 12.5 cm (5 in.) in length. Underwater photo from Eilat, Red Sea, at a depth of 10 m (33 ft).
Photo: Allen.

301.
Chaetodon paucifasciatus Subadult which vaguely shows a black spot on the posterior part of the dorsal fin. Juveniles up to a length of about 5 cm (2 in.) are distinctly marked with this spot.
Photo: Voigtmann.

300 ▲ 301 ▼

The Red-back Butterflyfish occurs only in the Red Sea and the adjacent Gulf of Aden. It is closely related to *C. mertensii* and *C. xanthurus* from the tropical Indo-West Pacific and *C. madagascariensis* from the Indian Ocean. It has a color pattern that is similar to *C. mertensii* (see Vol. 1), but the posterior portion of the body is red instead of yellow and the forehead spot is outlined with white (as in *C. xanthurus).* I have observed this species at Eilat and Jeddah, where it frequents coral and rubble areas at depths between four and 30 meters (13 and 100 ft). At Eilat, near the head of the Gulf of Aqaba, this species is commonly seen in pairs or small groups. It is relatively common on the section of reef adjacent to the public aquarium and is frequently sighted by visitors at the impressive undersea observation tower. It feeds on coral polyps, gorgonians, algae, polychaete worms, and small crustaceans. This attractive fish does well in aquarium surroundings and therefore is highly prized by hobbyists. The maximum size is approximately 14 cm (5.6 in.).

A Group of *Chaetodon paucifasciatus* in the Red Sea

302.
A small group of
*Chaetodon pauci-
fasciatus.* Underwater
photo from the Red
Sea.
Photo: Moosleitner.

Chaetodon quadrimaculatus
Fourspot Butterflyfish

GRAY, 1831

The Fourspot Butterflyfish has a distinctive appearance characterized by the presence of two white spots on the upper sides. It is an inhabitant of Oceania and has been recorded from the Hawaiian Islands, Johnston Atoll, Tuamotu Islands, Society Islands, Samoa, Phoenix Islands, Marshall Islands, Wake Island, and the Marianas. It does not appear to be particularly common at most localities except in certain parts of the Hawaiian Islands: for example, along the Kona coast on the island of Hawaii. The species is frequently seen in pairs and shows a fairly high degree of specialization in choice of habitat. It is rarely seen below 10 meters (33 ft) and is usually found considerably shallower. It prefers areas that are exposed to moderate or at least slight surge action; for example, on the leeward side of Oahu in the Hawaiian Islands it is encountered in rocky areas near Kaena Point at two to six meters (6.6 to 19.6 ft). It is frequently seen feeding on the polyps of *Pocillopora* coral heads. Young specimens are present along the rocky shores of the Hawaiian Islands between May and September. It is not a particularly good aquarium species and often exhibits shyness and reluctance to feed. The maximum size is 16 cm (6.4 in.).

303.
*Chaetodon
quadrimaculatus*
Adult individual,
13 cm (5 in.) in length.
Aquarium photo.
Photo:
Nieuwenhuizen.

Chaetodon robustus
Robust Butterflyfish

GÜNTHER, 1860

This species appears to be the most common butterflyfish along the tropical coast of West Africa. It usually inhabits rocky areas in a depth range extending from inshore shallows (one to two meters/ 3.3 to 6.6 ft) to at least 50 meters (164 ft). It is particularly common on rocky reefs of the northern Gulf of Guinea (i. e., Liberia to Nigeria). The species is often seen in pairs and is relatively easy to approach at close range. Few specimens have entered the aquarium trade, consequently there is little information on its maintenance in captivity. Many authors have referred to this species as *C. luciae* which is a synonym. The maximum size is about 17 cm (6.8 in.).

304.
Chaetodon robustus
Adult pair. Underwater photo from the Cape Verde Islands.
Photo: Gruhl.

305.
Chaetodon robustus
Also known by the name *C. luciae*. Juvenile from the Ghana coast. Underwater photo: Lubbock.

304 ▼

305 ▶

Chaetodon sanctaehelenae   GÜNTHER, 1868
St. Helena Butterflyfish

306 ▲   307 ▲   308 ▼

A School of *Chaetodon sanctaehelenae, Ascension, Atlantic Ocean*

This species is known only at St. Helena and Ascension islands, two small outposts located in the middle of the tropical Atlantic. It is said to be moderately common at Ascension and abundant at St. Helena, where it often gathers to feed on refuse dumped into the harbor. The species is most often seen in pairs, but groups of 20 to 30 fishes that feed on plankton up to several meters off the bottom are sometimes encountered. It prefers rocky areas at depths of one to two meters (3.3 to 6.6 ft) to at least 20 meters (66 ft).

Juvenile specimens have a black spot on the edge of the dorsal fin which gradually disappears with growth. In addition, the body has a slight silvery sheen and the outer margin of the anal fin is dusky. The maximum size is about 15 cm (6 in.). The species has not been kept in home aquaria.

306.
Chaetodon sanctaehelenae
Juvenile, about 4 cm (1.6 in.) in length. Ascension Island, Atlantic Ocean.
Photo: Lubbock.

307.
Chaetodon sanctaehelenae
Subadult. Underwater photo from Ascension, Atlantic Ocean.
Photo: Lubbock.

308.
Chaetodon sanctaehelenae
Adult. Underwater photo from Ascension, Atlantic Ocean.
Photo: Lubbock

309.
Chaetodon sanctaehelenae
Ascension, Atlantic Ocean. The coloration of these individuals differs slightly from that of specimens from St. Helena. The underwater shots of this species were made especially for this book by Roger Lubbock.

309

Chaetodon sedentarius
Reef Butterflyfish

POEY, 1860

310.
*Chaetodon
sedentarius*
Juvenile. 3.75 cm
(1.5 in.).
Aquarium photo.
Photo: Norman.

311.
*Chaetodon
sedentarius*
Subadult. Underwater
photo from Rose Is-
land, Bahamas at a
depth of one meter
(3.3 ft).
Photo: Baensch.

The Reef Butterflyfish is an inhabitant of the eastern Gulf of Mexico and the Caribbean Sea. It also ranges northward along the east coast of the United States as far as North Carolina. It is relatively common in some offshore reef areas of southern Florida and, according to Böhlke and Chaplin (1968), the least abundant *Chaetodon* in the Bahamas. Hans Baensch observed and photographed two juveniles of 2 to 5 cm (0.4 to 2 in.) in length east of Rose Island, Nassau (Bahamas) at a depth between 50 cm and one meter (1.6 and 3.3 ft). It is found on coral reefs, usually at greater depths than most of the West Indian butterflyfishes; the exceptions are *C. aya, C. guyanensis,* and *C. aculeatus.* The normal depth range is about 15 to at least 40 meters (50 to 130 ft). This species is frequently available to hobbyists in the United States and occasionally appears on the European market. It is a relatively hardy species that does well in captivity. The natural diet contains such items as polychaete worms, shrimps, amphipods, and hydroids. Juvenile specimens possess an ocellated spot on the soft dorsal fin. The maximum size is about 15 cm (6 in.).

310 ▲   311 ▼

312 ▼

312.
*Chaetodon
sedentarius*
Subadult. Under-
water photo from
Triumph Reef, Florida.
Photo: Thresher.

313.
*Chaetodon
sedentarius*
Underwater photo of
an adult from the Ber-
muda Islands.
Photo: Colin.

313 ▼

Chaetodon semilarvatus
Golden Butterflyfish

While diving in the Red Sea off Jeddah in 1976 I encountered a school of approximately 20 Golden Butterflies. The beauty of these fishes was absolutely astounding and that dive will always remain as one of my most memorable. The combination of large size, brilliant colors, and graceful swimming movements make this species one of the most attractive members of the family. It is found only in the Red Sea and normally frequents areas of rich coral growth at depths of four to 20 meters (13 to 66 ft). It is most often seen in pairs or small aggregations. Occasionally this fish is observed hovering in a stationary position for extended periods under ledges formed by *Acropora* plate corals. This species is usually fearless, and thus it is possible to approach at close

range. It is periodically exported to Europe and America, and the smaller specimens do well in aquarium surroundings. Adults reach a maximum size of about 30 cm (12 in.) and therefore are much too large for the average household aquarium. Small specimens quickly adapt to aquarium conditions and will survive in captivity for four to six years.

314 ▼

314.
Chaetodon semilarvatus
Adults from the Red Sea. The animal in the foreground shows an unusual variation stripe pattern.
Photo: Roediger.

315. (next page)
A group of *Chaetodon semilarvatus* grazing in the coral garden of a reef in the Red Sea.
Photo: Voigtmann.

Chaetodon smithi
Smith's Butterflyfish

RANDALL, 1975

This unusual bicolored species was recently discovered in the remote southeast corner of Polynesia. It was first seen by Dr. Dennis Devaney, a marine invertebrate biologist from the Bishop Museum in Honolulu during an expedition to Pitcairn Island in 1967. Three years later the first specimens were procured at the island of Rapa by Dr. C. Lavett Smith of the American Museum of Natural History, and only a few months later Dr. John Randall of the Bishop Museum visited Rapa and Pitcairn aboard the sailing ship *Westward* on an expedition sponsored by the National Geographic Society. He collected approximately one dozen specimens and eventually described the species as *C. smithi* in honor of the first collector. This species is known only at the islands of Pitcairn,

Rapa, and Îlots de Bass (Marotiri), a group of ten rocky islets 80 km (50 miles) southeast of Rapa. It is particularly abundant on the reefs and rocky shores of Rapa and large aggregations were sometimes encountered by Dr. Randall. Because of its limited distribution in an area well off the beaten track, it is highly unlikely that this species will be introduced to the aquarium trade. The maximum size is about 17 cm (6.8 in.).

316 ▼

Chaetodon smithi, Rapa, S. Pacific

316.
Chaetodon smithi
Adults. It is difficult to photograph this species under water because of the contrasting colors.
Photo: Randall.

317.
Chaetodon smithi
When danger threatens the school retreats to the surface of the reef. The predominance of algae is characteristic of subtropical and temperate reefs.
Photo: Randall.

317 ▲   318 ▼

318.
Chaetodon smithi
A mid-water plankton feeder, with habits similar to the species of *Hemitaurichthys.*
Photo: Randall.

Chaetodon striatus
Banded Butterflyfish

LINNAEUS, 1758

319 ▲

Chaetodon striatus, one of the first butterflyfishes to be described, was included in *Systema Naturae* by the famous Swedish naturalist Carole Linnaeus. This monumental work was published in 1758 and represents the first official use of our present day system of binominal nomenclature (i. e., genus and species). The Banded Butterflyfish occurs on both sides of the tropical Atlantic. In the western Atlantic it ranges from Brazil northward to the Caribbean Sea and Gulf of Mexico. It is also found along the east coast of the United States as far north as Massachusetts due to larval transport via the warm Gulf Stream. It is generally common on most West Indian coral reefs, solitarily or in pairs, at depths of three to 20 meters (10 to 66 ft). Randall (1967), in an examination of the gut contents of 16 specimens from Puerto Rico and the Virgin Islands, noted that the diet of this species includes polychaete worms (sabellids, serpulids, and terebillids) and coral polyps. Lesser amounts of unidentified crustaceans and mollusc eggs were also found. The Banded Butterflyfish is frequently available from marine fish dealers and although not particularly colorful its handsome pattern of brown and white and its peaceful nature make it a desirable aquarium addition. Small juveniles possess an ocellated spot on the soft dorsal fin which gradually disappears with growth. The maximum size is about 16 cm (6.4 in.). Weber and De Beaufort (1936) described *Anisochaetodon trivirgatus* on the basis of a single specimen supposedly collected at Ambon in the Molucca Islands of Indonesia. This species, however, is most certainly *C. striatus* from the Atlantic. Evidently an error was made in labeling this specimen or perhaps separate collections from the Atlantic and Pacific were inadvertently mixed at the Amsterdam Museum, where the specimen is deposited.

320 ▼

319.
Chaetodon striatus
Juvenile. Underwater photo taken at a depth of one meter (3.3 ft). New Providence, Bahamas.
Photo: Baensch.

320.
Chaetodon striatus
Adult. Aquarium photo.
Photo: Kahl.

Chaetodon striatus on the Reef, Bahamas

321.
Chaetodon striatus
Adult pair from Love
Beach, New Provi-
dence, Bahamas, at a
depth of 5 m (16 ft).
This species is often
found among gorgo-
nian branches.
Photo: Baensch

Chaetodon tinkeri
Tinker's Butterflyfish

SCHULTZ, 1951

Tinker's Butterflyfish occurs only in the Hawaiian Islands. It is probably more common than generally believed, but because it frequents depths greater than those usually visited by divers it is seldom seen. Most of the sightings have come from depths between 40 and 75 meters (130–246 ft). It is often found in the vicinity of steep slopes, solitary or in pairs and occasionally in small aggregations. Its diet includes a variety of planktonic and benthic organisms, and partly for this reason *C. tinkeri* does well in captivity in contrast to many butterflyfishes that are more specialized in their feeding and are frequently restricted to browsing on coral polyps. In a recent study published by Randall, Allen, and Steene (1977) a hybrid butterflyfish which represents a cross between *C. tinkeri* and *C. miliaris* was described. The hybrid is known on the basis of three specimens, 41 to 60 mm (1.6 to 2.4 in.) in standard length. It exhibits a blend of color pattern characters from each parent; for example, faint spotting on the sides is derived from *miliaris* and a partly darkened area posteriorly is derived from *C. tinkeri*. The maximum size for *C. tinkeri* is about 15 cm (6 in.). The species is closely related to *C. declivis* Randall from the Marquesas Islands.

322 ▲

323 ▼

322.
Chaetodon tinkeri
11 cm (4.4 in.).
Aquarium photo.
Photo: Norman.

323.
Chaetodon tinkeri
13 cm (5 in.).
Aquarium photo.
Photo:
Nieuwenhuizen.

Chaetodon triangulum
Triangular Butterflyfish

CUVIER, 1831

This species is similar to *C. baronessa* of the western Pacific which was featured in Vol. 1. The best means of distinguishing the two is the coloration of the caudal fin. *C. baronessa* has a narrow dark band across the middle of the fin, but in *triangulum* this band is greatly expanded and occupies most of the tail. It is roughly diamond shaped. *C. triangulum* is primarily an Indian Ocean species, but it also occurs around some of the islands in the western sector of the Indonesian Archipelago; for example, it has entered the Java Sea via the Sunda Strait and is found on the north coast of Java and at the Seribu Islands, which lie a short distance off Jakarta. The species is most often encountered in pairs at depths ranging between about three and 15 meters (10 and 50 ft). It is closely associated with *Acropora* corals, particularly the staghorn variety. It is mainly a coral polyp feeder and therefore does not adjust easily to aquarium conditions. The maximum size is about 15 cm (6 in.). This species was formerly included in the genus *Gonochaetodon.*

324.
Chaetodon triangulum
Adult individual. The characteristic coloration of the caudal fin is easily seen. The species is closely related to *Chaetodon baronessa,* Vol. 1, page 16.
Photo: Nieuwenhuizen.

Chaetodon trichrous
Tahiti Butterflyfish

GÜNTHER, 1874

325 ▲   326 ▼

This species is native to the Society Islands. There is also a record of its occurrence at Palmyra, some 2500 km (1563 miles) to the north in the Line Islands. The Palmyra record, however, may be due to a labeling error or misidentification and needs to be substantiated by further collecting. This species does not appear to be particularly abundant. Few individuals were seen around the island of Bora Bora during a visit there in 1969. It was more common at Tahiti and a number of specimens were sighted in shallow lagoons that lie behind the protection of the outer fringing reef. It usually appears singly or in pairs, but occasionally small aggregations of four to six fish are encountered. This species bears a remarkable resemblance to the angelfish *Chaetodontoplus mesoleucus,* particularly in color pattern, but the angelfish is easily distinguished by the presence of a stout, sharp spine on the lower edge of the cheek. Moreover, it is confined to the Indo-Australian Archipelago and therefore is not likely to be confused with *trichrous.* Because of the relatively somber color pattern and limited distribution, the Tahiti Butterflyfish is seldom exported, although small specimens seem to adjust well to captivity. The maximum size is about 12 cm (4.8 in.).

325.
Chaetodon trichrous
Adult. Underwater photo from Tahiti.
Photo: Lubbock.

326.
Chaetodon trichrous
Adult of 10 cm (4 in.) in length. An individual from Teavaraa Tass, Tahiti, at a depth of 15 m (50 ft).
Photo: Randall.

Chaetodon unimaculatus
Teardrop Butterflyfish

BLOCH, 1787

This well-known species has a wide distribution that extends from the Hawaiian Islands westward across the vast tropical Indo-Pacific region to the coast of East Africa. It was featured in Vol. 1, but because of the variability of its color pattern it is included here. Specimens from Australia and the Pacific islands generally exhibit a white ground color (see Vol. 1, p. 51), whereas those from the Indian Ocean and western portion of the Indo-Malayan Archipelago are often brilliant yellow. In addition, the eye bar of the Indian Ocean variety is narrower. This pattern is note-worthy because most members of the family show little variation in color throughout their range. Some authorities, such as Burgess (1978), recognize two subspecies, *C. unimaculatus interruptus* from the Indian Ocean and *C. unimaculatus unimaculatus* from the Pacific. The Teardrop Butterflyfish is often seen in pairs or small groups at depths of about four to 20 meters (13 to 66 ft). In the Hawaiian Islands it is commonly encountered below five meters (16 ft) in rocky areas that contain scattered heads of *Pocillopora* coral or in areas of rich *Porites* growths. Juveniles are present along rocky shores in the Hawaiian Islands during the summer months. These smaller specimens are particularly handsome and do well in captivity. The adults reach a maximum size of about 20 cm (8 in.). Randall, Allen, and Steene (1977) reported a hybrid cross between this species and *C. kleinii* from Enewetak Atoll.

327.
Chaetodon unimaculatus
The yellow form that occurs in the Indian Ocean.
Photo: Roediger.

328.
A pair of *Chaetodon unimaculatus* from the coast of Sri Lanka. Underwater photo at a depth of 10 m (3.3 ft).
Photo: Debelius.

327 ▼   328 ▶

Chaetodon wiebeli
Wiebel's Butterflyfish

329 ▲

330 ▼

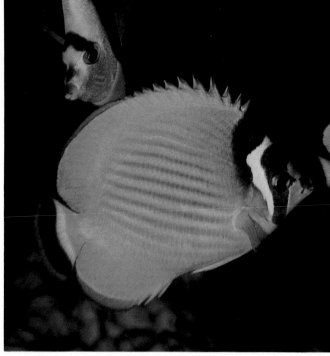

329.
Chaetodon wiebeli
Adults. These fish live in a large circular show aquarium with a diameter of 12 m (39.3 ft) at Seapark, Hongkong.
Photo: Baensch.

330.
Chaetodon wiebeli
Adult. Photographed at Seapark, Hong-kong.
Photo: Baensch.

This distinctive species is characterized by a golden-orange coloration with a series of reddish-brown, obliquely ascending bands on the sides. The head markings are particularly diagnostic. The species has sometimes been referred to as *C. bellamaris* Seale. It occurs primarily along the eastern Asian coast from Japan to Thailand. The northernmost record is from the Kochi Prefecture on Shikoku Island, southern Japan. The distribution also embraces the Ryukyu Islands, Taiwan, South China Sea, and the Gulf of Thailand. The species generally inhabits coral reefs at depths ranging from about four meters (13 ft) to at least 25 meters (82 ft). It is usually solitary but sometimes occurs in pairs. A complete black band which extends from the nape to the lower edge of the gill cover, an ocellated spot on the soft dorsal fin, and a black band across the tail base are juvenile features not found in adults. With growth the head band is gradually divided in two leaving an isolated portion on the nape. The maximum size of adults is about 18 cm (7.2 in.). This species thrives in captivity. Part of the diet consists of feeding on algal covered stones.

Chaetodon xanthocephalus
Yellowhead Butterflyfish

BENNETT, 1832

This species is widely distributed in the western Indian Ocean. Its range extends along the East African coast from Somalia as far south as Durban. It is also found at Sri Lanka, Maldives, Chagos Archipelago, Seychelles, Madagascar, and Mauritius. Normally, it is solitary, but it also occurs in pairs at depths of five to 25 meters (16 to 82 ft). It prefers areas that have a high percentage of live corals covering the bottom. It is morphologically similar to *C. ephippium* and there is evidence that hybrid crosses are sometimes made between them. Burgess (1974) illustrated a possible hybrid from Sri Lanka, which had the general shape and coloration of *C. xanthocephalus* except for the large black marking on the upper back and posterior dorsal fin typical of *C. ephippium.* Although it is only occasionally exported this species appears to thrive in captivity, but sometimes there are initial difficulties. The small juveniles have a large black area that covers most of the posterior portion of the dorsal fin and there is also a prominent black spot at the base of the tail. The maximum size is about 20 cm (8 in.).

331 ▲

332 ▲

333 ▼

332.
*Chaetodon
xanthocephalus*
Juvenile of 5 cm (2 in.)
in length. Aquarium
photo.
Photo: Norman.

331.
*Chaetodon
xanthocephalus*
Night coloration.
Underwater photo
from Tanzania, Africa.
Adult individual.
Photo: Kipper.

333.
*Chaetodon
xanthocephalus*
Adult pair.
Kenya, Africa.
Photo: Kipper.

Chaetodon xanthurus
Yellow-Tail Butterflyfish

BLEEKER, 1857

This species is closely related to *C. mertensii* (Vol. 1, p. 30), *C. madagascariensis,* and *C. paucifasciatus.* The members of this species complex have similar color patterns but can be easily differentiated. *Chaetodon xanthurus* is the only member of the group with a crosshatch pattern of dark lines on the sides. There appears to be little overlap in the distributions of these allied species; *C. xanthurus* is present in the East Indies, the Philippines, and Okinawa; *C. mertensii* is a Pacific Ocean species that ranges eastward to the Tuamotus; *C. madagascariensis* is widespread in the Indian Ocean; and *C. paucifasciatus* is endemic to the Red Sea. The Yellow-Tail Butterflyfish is generally seen below a 15 meter (49 ft) depth and occurs alone or in pairs. It is frequently exported as an aquarium fish from the Philippine Islands and appears to be well suited for life in captivity. The maximum size is about 14 cm (5.6 in.).

334.
Chaetodon xanthurus
Adult pair photograph-
ed in an aquarium.
Photo:
Nieuwenhuizen.

Chaetodon zanzibariensis
Zanzibar Butterflyfish

PLAYFAIR, 1866

This species bears a slight resemblance to *Chaetodon speculum*. However, it has a series of faint stripes on the sides and the black spot on the upper back is at least partly margined with a silvery white or bluish color. In addition, the spot tends to be smaller than in *speculum*. *C. zanzibariensis* is distributed along the coast of East Africa. It is relatively common on certain reefs near the city of Dar es Salaam, Tanzania, at which locality it is usually seen alone or in pairs but occasionally in small groups, particularly in the vicinity of staghorn *Acropora* thickets. The usual

depth range extends from about three to 14 meters (10 to 46 ft). Much of the diet of this species consists of live coral; therefore it is difficult to maintain for any length of time in captivity. The maximum size is about 12 cm (4.8 in.).

335.
*Chaetodon
zanzibariensis*
Adult about 13 cm
(5 in.) photographed
underwater at Mahé,
Seychelles.
Photo: Allen.

335 ▼

336.
*Chaetodon
zanzibariensis*
Juvenile, 6 cm (2.4 in.)
in length. Aquarium
photo.
Photo: Myers.

336 ▶

Genus: *Hemitaurichthys*

Hemitaurichthys multispinosus
Many-Spined Butterflyfish

RANDALL, 1975

This species is known only from the tiny island of Pitcairn. Although this isolated volcanic outcrop has a fascinating marine biota, it is better known as the refuge of Fletcher Christian and his band of mutineers from Captain Bligh's ship *Bounty.* The descendants of her crew still live on the island and many retain the surnames of their famous ancestors. The Many-Spined Butterflyfish was first collected in January 1971 by Dr. John E. Randall during an expedition of the National Geographic Society to southeast Oceania. It appears to be a deep-dwelling species and was collected and observed only on a small section of well-developed coral reef known as "The Bear", which lies off Gannett Ridge on the north side of Pitcairn. Nine specimens were taken at this locality with spears and rotenone poison. One of Dr. Randall's collecting assistants was Steve Christian, a descendant of the famous mutineer. The specimens were taken at depths ranging between 40 and 44 meters (130 and 144 ft). *H. multispinosus* is similar in appearance to *H. thompsoni,* but is more elongate and has more dorsal spines (15 or 16 compared with 12 for *thompsoni*). The unusually high number of dorsal spines prompted Dr. Randall to name this species *multispinosus* (Latin for "many spines"). The maximum size is about 20 cm (8 in.).

337.
Hemitaurichthys multispinosus
Adult, SL 14.8 cm (5.9 in.). From Pitcairn Island, at a depth of 45 m (148 ft).
Photo: Randall.

Hemitaurichthys thompsoni
Thompson's Butterflyfish

FOWLER, 1923

This species is easily identified by its drab coloration and lack of distinguishing markings. The ground color ranges from dark grey to nearly black. *H. thompsoni* is a relatively rare species with a limited distribution. It is found in the Hawaiian Islands and at Johnston Island, an isolated atoll about 700 km (438 miles) south of the Hawaiian chain. It is locally common in some areas of Hawaii, particularly at Molokini Rock off the island of Maui, and along the Kona coast on the island of Hawaii. It frequently forms midwater aggregations, which apparently feed on zooplankton. Single individuals or pairs are sometimes sighted on shallow coral reefs which are adjacent to deep water. The normal depth range is approximately 12 to 40 meters (39 to 130 ft), but at Johnston Island small groups are sometimes encountered in lagoon areas at depths as shallow as five to 10 meters (16 to 33 ft). It is not a particularly shy fish and may be approached at close range. This species is not well known in the aquarium trade because of its general scarcity in nature and lack of vivid coloration. Small specimens, however, do well in captivity on a standard diet which includes occasional feedings of live brine shrimp. The maximum size is about 18 cm (7.2 in.). Small juveniles generally resemble the adults but are rarely seen.

338.
Hemitaurichthys thompsoni
Adult from Hawaii, at a depth of 12 m (39 ft).
Photo: Allen.

339.
Hemitaurichthys thompsoni
Adult. 12.5 cm (5 in.). Kona, Hawaii, at a depth of 10 m (33 ft).
Photo: Allen.

338 ▲

339 ▼

Hemitaurichthys zoster
Black Pyramid Butterflyfish

(BENNETT, 1831)

This species is similar to *H. polylepis* of the western Pacific but differs markedly in coloration. Both species have a white pyramid-shaped area that covers the central portion of the body, but in *H. zoster* the remainder of the body is primarily dark brown or blackish instead of yellow as in *H. polylepis* (see Vol. 1). The Black-Pyramid Butterflyfish is found around island areas in the western Indian Ocean. In the Maldive Islands it is common on some reefs adjacent to deep water at depths ranging from about 10 to at least 35 meters (33 to 115 ft). It frequently forms huge schools of several hundred individuals that feed on planktonic organisms high above the bottom. When danger threatens, for example at the approach of a diver, the school quickly retreats to the protec-

tive shelter of the reef. Although seldom exported, this species does well in captivity, but should be given live foods such as brine shrimp nauplii on a regular basis. The maximum size is about 16 cm (6.4 in.).

340 ▼

340.
Hemitaurichthys zoster
Adult. Underwater photo from the Maldive Islands.
Photo: Voigtmann.

341.
Hemitaurichthys zoster
This large school was photographed at a depth of 20 m (66 ft) in the Maldive Islands.
Photo: Voigtmann.

Genus: *Heniochus*

Bannerfishes

Heniochus intermedius
Red Sea Bannerfish

STEINDACHNER, 1893

342 ▲

342.
Heniochus intermedius
Juvenile, nearly 10 cm
(4 in.) in length.
Aquarium photo.
Photo: Norman.

343.
Heniochus intermedius
Red Sea. Underwater
photo at a depth of
15 m (50 ft). The spe-
cies grows to a length
of 18 cm (7.2 in.).
Photo: Roediger.

Several authors have considered this species to be a synonym of *H. acuminatus* . Klausewitz (1969), however, correctly recognized it as a distinct species. It is found only in the Red Sea where it co-occurs with *H. diphreutes*. These two species can be separated easily on the basis of color pattern and differences in ecology and behavior. *H. intermedius* is generally associated with coral reefs and is most often seen alone or in pairs but occasionally in aggregations. On the contrary, *H. diphreutes* usually occurs in large swarms over sandy or rocky areas in bays, lagoons, and estuaries. According to Klausewitz, the young of *intermedius* form large groups in the deeper zones of the reef where there are no living corals. During the juvenile stages this species is sometimes found in mixed schools with *H. diphreutes*. The overall yellowish suffusion and faint coloration of the dark bars on its upper body are characters that facilitate rapid identification of *intermedius*. The species is common in the Gulf of Aqaba and is very easy to approach at close range on the coral reef adjacent to the public aquarium at Eilat. At this same locality I photographed an unusual specimen with two elongate dorsal filaments. This species does well in the aquarium, accepting a variety of live and fresh frozen foods in addition to dried commercial preparations. The maximum size is about 18 cm (7.2 in.).

343 ▼

344.
The underwater photo
of this school of
Heniochus intermedius
was taken in the Red
Sea, at a depth of
about 10 m (33 ft).
Photo: Moosleitner.

A School of *Heniochus intermedius* in the Red Sea

Heniochus pleurotaenia
Indian Bannerfish

AHL, 1923

345.
*Heniochus
pleurotaenia*
Subadult. Under-
water photo from the
Maldive Islands.
Photo: Voigtmann.

346.
*Heniochus
pleurotaenia*
Adult. Underwater
photo from the Mal-
dive Islands.
Photo: Langhoff.

345 ▲   346 ▼

Until recently *H. pleurotaenia* was known only from Sumatra and was thought to be a junior synonym of *H. varius* (see Vol. 1). Klausewitz (1969) revised *Heniochus* and presented evidence to indicate that it is indeed a valid species. The distribution includes Java, Sumatra, Nicobar Islands, Sri Lanka, and the Maldive Islands. The bony projection on the nape is a feature found on both *H. pleuro-taenia* and *H. varius,* but the two are easily separated by color pattern; *pleurotaenia* has an extra white band that originates at the base of the anal spines and extends to the middle of the upper sides. Both species are inhabitants of coral reefs, but *H. varius* is usually seen alone or in pairs in contrast to *H. pleurotaenia* which is frequently encountered in aggrega-tions of 20 to 30 individuals. The normal depth distribution extends from two to three meters (6.6 to 10 ft) to about 20 meters (66 ft). This species is occasionally imported, but does not appear to be as hardy as some of the other bannerfishes such as *H. acumi-natus* and *H. diphreutes.* The maximum size is about 18 cm (7.2 in.).

Genus: *Johnrandallia*

Johnrandallia nigrirostris
Barberfish

(GILL, 1862)

Johnrandallia nigrirostris, an inhabitant of the tropical eastern Pacific, ranges from Baja California as far south as Mapelo Island off Colombia. This species has been included in the genus *Heniochus* by most authors, but in overall appearance it is clearly different from the other members of that group. It is most closely allied to *Chaetodon* but differs from all other species in this genus by possessing a complete lateral line. Nalbant (1974) described the genus *Johnrandallia* which contains only *nigrirostris.* Burgess (1978) was apparently unaware of Nalbant's description when he placed this species in a new genus, *Pseudochaetodon.* It is the most common species of butterflyfish in the Gulf of California. Its normal depth range is about four to five meters (13 to 16 ft) to at least 40 meters (130 ft). The common name of this species is derived from its habit of engaging in symbiotic cleaning behavior with other fishes. Among Mexican fishermen it is known as "El Barbero", which simply translates as "the barber". According to a report by Mr. Alex Kerstitch of the University of Arizona, well established cleaning stations are attended by a number of different reef species. While being cleaned they remain motionless as the Barberfish picks off infected bits of skin and ectoparasites. In some cases more than 100 fishes congregate at these undersea barber shops, each patiently waiting its turn to be inspected by *J. nigrirostris.* Occasionally large schools of 100 or more Barberfish engage in mass cleaning activities. Thus it appears that this species plays an important role in maintaining the overall health of the local fish community. Its unusual habits and attractive appearance make this species a welcome addition to a marine aquarium. The maximum size is about 16 cm (6.4 in.).

347.
Johnrandallia nigrirostris
Underwater photo of an adult fish from Baja California, Mexico, at a depth of about 30 m (100 ft). Photo: Hall.

Family
Pomacanthidae

Angelfishes

Introduction

The angelfish family Pomacanthidae contains 74 species that inhabit tropical seas around the world. Most are found in the vicinity of coral reefs where they usually occur as solitary individuals or in small groups. Many of the species inhabit relatively shallow water in depths just below the influence of strong surge (usually two to three meters, 6.6 to 10 ft) down to 10 to 15 meters (33 to 49 ft). Others however, are restricted to rather deep water; for example, some of the *Centropyge* and *Genicanthus* are seldom seen in less than 20 meters (66 ft) and may range to 50 meters (164 ft) or deeper. Angelfishes are well known for their dazzling color patterns and many species, particularly those belonging to *Pomacanthus* and *Holacanthus,* exhibit dramatic changes from the juvenile to adult stage.

Zoogeography

Angelfishes occur in all tropical seas, but most of the species inhabit the species-rich Indo-Pacific region. Indeed, all but nine species, or approximately 88% of the total number, are found in this vast area. The far western edge of the Pacific Ocean contains about 40 species, far more than any other region. Thus it is not surprising that the countries with the richest pomacanthid faunas all lie within this area. The five leading countries are as follows (number of species in parentheses): 1. Australia (23); 2. New Guinea (22); 3. Indonesia (21); 4. Taiwan (20); 5. Philippine Islands (19).

Six of the species have very broad distributions that range over most of the western Pacific westward to the coast of East Africa. Twelve have ranges that cover parts of the Indian Ocean, including two species which are restricted to the Red Sea and adjacent Gulf of Aden. Nine are found in the tropical Atlantic, all except *Holacanthus africanus* and *Centropyge resplendens* mainly in the western portion. The eastern tropical Pacific is the home of four angelfishes. The remaining species are basically western Pacific forms, although some have rather restricted ranges that cover only a small portion of this vast region. Although somewhat confusing, the west coast of Australia, Christmas Island, and the Cocos-Keeling group, all of which lie at the eastern edge of the

Indian Ocean, are actually part of the West Pacific faunal region. Five angelfishes have extremely limited ranges confined to a single small island or island group: *Apolemichthys guezei* (Réunion), *Centropyge colini* (Cocos-Keeling Islands), *Centropyge resplendens* (Ascension Island), *Genicanthus semifasciatus* (Lord Howe Island), and *Holacanthus limbaughi* (Clipperton Island).

Biology

Most of the angelfish species are greatly dependent on the presence of shelter in the form of boulders, caves, and coral crevices and are seldom seen over vast sandy stretches or other areas of low relief. Typically, most species are somewhat territorial and spend most of the time near the bottom in search of food, periodically retreating to shelter within the reef. Members of the genus *Genicanthus,* however, are characteristically open water swimmers and often form aggregations that forage on plankton well above the bottom.

Food-habit studies have been conducted for several species. Apparently there are three basic feeding types within the family. Many of the smaller species, particularly of *Centropyge,* feed almost exclusively on algae. This item was by far the dominant food source for *C. flavissimus* in a study by Hiatt and Strasburg (1960). Randall (1967) also reported an algal diet for *C. argi.* Many, if not all, of the large angelfishes belonging to *Pomacanthus* and *Holacanthus* feed on sponges supplemented by algae and small amounts of zoantharians, tunicates, gorgonians, various eggs, hydroids, and spermatophytes (including seagrasses). The spongefeeding habits of Atlantic angelfishes have been well documented by Randall and Hartman (1968). The third major feeding method among angelfishes is displayed by the species of *Genicanthus.* As already mentioned, they frequently form midwater aggregations that feed largely on pelagic tunicates supplemented by benthic items such as bryozoans, polychaetes, and algae.

Perhaps one of strangest dietary items recorded for an angelfish involves the Japanese species *Centropyge interruptus.* Moyer and Nakazono (1978) noted that individuals studied at Miyake-jima received a significant amount of their nourishment by

eating the feces of planktonfeeding damselfishes (Pomacentridae) and fairy basslets *(Anthias).*
There has, in general, been a scarcity of information about the courtship and reproductive habits of angelfishes. The recent (1978) study by Moyer and Nakazono, however, is an exception and provides us with much valuable data which may be applicable to many other members of the family. These authors investigated the reproductive habits of *Centropyge interruptus,* a species that occurs typically in harems that contain a single dominant male and one to four females; these harems exhibit a sort of peck-order or hierarchical system of dominance. Their size is controlled by the nature of the sub-stratum. The largest are found in areas in which intricate caverns and ledges provide maximum shelter. Boulder habitats, on the other hand, offer minimal shelter and are usually occupied by nonpermanent pairs. If the male is experimentally removed from the harem, a remarkable alteration occurs in the top-ranking female; it gradually changes to the male sex over a period of only two to three weeks in a transformation of ovarian tissues into functional testes accompanied by color changes on the head and fins. Similar cases of sex inversion have been documented for *Genicanthus semifasciatus* by Shen and Liu (1975) and for *G. lamarck* by Suzuki *et. al.* (reported by Moyer and Nakazono, 1978). It appears that harem formation and possible sex inversion may be widespread among the species of *Centropyge* and *Genicanthus;* for example, Moyer and Nakazono have observed harems in *C. vroliki, C. heraldi, C. flavissimus, C. ferrugatus,* and *C. tibicen.* Nevertheless, the monogamous pair appears to be the reproductive unit of the large *Pomacanthus* and many of the *Holacanthus* angels; it is not known if they are capable of sex inversion. Spawning in *Centropyge interruptus* at Miyake-jima generally occurs daily between May and October and seems to be controlled by temperature and light conditions. Spawning will not take place if the water temperature drops below 22° C (72° F). Moyer and Nakazono observed 175 spawnings and the majority of these occurred between 10 minutes before and 5 minutes after sunset, unless the day was heavily overcast. In that case the activities commenced much earlier. Courtship behavior consists of rapid

rushing and circling of individual females by the male. In the final stages before actual spawning the male characteristically exhibits a "soaring" display in which he swims high off the bottom above a female and then strikes a motionless pose with all the fins extended. Eventually the female approaches at close range and is "nuzzled" around the abdominal region by the male. This behavior leads to a sudden spawning burst in which eggs and sperm are simultaneously released in open water. Both partners then quickly retreat to the bottom. The male usually spawns with each female member of the harem during one session in a spawning period that lasts only eight to ten minutes. The eggs are buoyant and float to the surface where they are planktonic for an undetermined period. Moe (1977) reported a hatching time for western Atlantic angelfish eggs of 18 to 30 hours.

Taxonomy

Most recent authors have followed the example of Fraser-Brunner (1933) in recognizing the angelfishes as a subfamily of the Chaetodontidae. There is firm evidence, however, based on internal and external morphology, for granting them separate family status (see Freihofer, 1963 and Burgess, 1974). The most obvious external feature that is useful for separating the two families is the prominent spine at the angle of the cheek which is present in angelfishes and absent in butterflyfishes. Another noteworthy difference involves the morphology of the larval stage. The body of chaetodontid larvae is covered with strange bony plates and the young are referred to as *Tholichthys*. In contrast, these plates are completely lacking in the larval stage of angelfishes.

The only recent comprehensive treatment of angelfishes is the paper published in 1933 by Fraser-Brunner. Most subsequent workers have followed his classification, although there has been some controversy, particularly in the last few years, in regard to the separation between *Holacanthus* and *Centropyge,* and between *Holacanthus* and *Genicanthus.* Admittedly, the differences between these genera are slight and therefore some authors prefer to lump the three in *Holacanthus.* Basically I have followed Fraser-Brunner's classification, but I have adopted Smith's (1955) recognition of *Apolemichthys* (a subgenus of *Holacanthus* according to Fraser-Brunner) and have placed *Heteropyge* (sometimes referred to as *Euxiphipops)* in the synonymy of *Pomacanthus* following Shen and Liu (1979).

FAMILY POMACANTHIDAE − 74 species

Subfamily Pomacanthinae
Genus *Chaetodontoplus* −
   9 species (far W. Pacific)
Genus *Pomacanthus*
  Subgenus *Arusetta* −
   1 species (Red Sea)
  Subgenus *Euxiphipops* −
   3 species (far W. Pacific)
  Subgenus *Pomacanthodes* −
   7 species (Indo-Pacific)
  Subgenus *Pomacanthus* −
   2 species (Atlantic)

Subfamily Holacanthinae
Genus *Apolemichthys* −
   6 species (Indo-West Pacific)
Genus *Centropyge*
  Subgenus *Centropyge* −
   10 species (Indo-West Pacific)
  Subgenus *Xiphipops* −
   18 species (Atlantic and Indo-West Pacific)
Genus *Genicanthus* −
   9 species (Indo-West Pacific)
Genus *Holacanthus*
  Subgenus *Angelichthys* −
   3 species (Atlantic)
  Subgenus *Holacanthus* −
   1 species (W. Atlantic)

  Subgenus, undetermined
   1 species *(H. venustus,* W. Pacific)
  Subgenus *Plitops* −
   3 species (E. Pacific)
Genus *Pygoplites* −
   1 species (Indo-West Pacific)

The main features that characterize the genera are briefly outlined in the following section (from Fraser-Brunner, 1933 and Shen and Liu, 1979).

The Species of Angelfishes, Family *Pomacanthidae* (Summary of Volumes 1 and 2)

The following list is based largely on the work of Fraser-Brunner (1933). Valid species appear in boldface type, synonyms in italics and indent. The approximate geographic distribution is given for valid species. Page numbers refer to Volumes 1 and 2 of **Butterfly and Angelfishes.**

Genus *Apolemichthys* Fraser-Brunner, 1933

Similar to *Holacanthus,* but preorbital convex without strong spines; also interoperculum without strong spines and preopercular spine not deeply grooved; scales on cheek small and irregular.

Apolemichthys arcuatus (Gray, 1831) – Hawaiian Islands, Vol. 2, p. 253

Apolemichthys guezei (Randall, 1978) – Réunion, Vol. 2, p. 254

> *Holacanthus guezei* Randall, 1978

Apolemichthys trimaculatus (Lacépède, in Cuvier, 1831) – Indo-West Pacific, Vol. 1, p. 92

> *Apolemichthys armitagei* Smith, 1955

Apolemichthys xanthopunctatus Burgess, 1973 – Central-W. Pacific, Vol. 2, p. 255

Apolemichthys xanthotis (Fraser-Brunner, 1951) – Red Sea and Gulf of Aden, Vol. 2, p. 256

Apolemichthys xanthurus (Bennett, 1832) – Sri Lanka and India, Vol. 2, p. 258

Genus *Centropyge* Kaup, 1860

Scales relatively large; interoperculum, small and serrated or with posterior spines; lateral line terminating at end of soft dorsal; hind margin of preorbital free.

Subgenus *Centropyge*

Centropyge aurantius Randall and Wass, 1974 – W. Pacific, Vol. 1, p. 94

Centropyge bicolor (Bloch, 1787) – W. Pacific, Vol. 1, p. 95

> *Holacanthus tenigab* Thiollière, 1857

Centropyge colini Smith-Vaniz and Randall, 1974 – Cocos-Keeling Islands, Vol. 2, p. 262

Centropyge eibli Klausewitz, 1963 – E. Indian Ocean, Vol. 1, p. 100

Centropyge flavissimus (Cuvier, 1831) – W. Pacific, Vol. 1, p. 102.

> *Holacanthus luteolus* Cuvier, 1831

> *Holacanthus cyanotis* Günther, 1860
> *Holacanthus monopthalmus* Kner, 1867
> *Holacanthus ocularis* Peters, 1868
> *Holacanthus sphynx* De Vis, 1884
> *Holacanthus uniocellatus* Borodin, 1932

Centropyge heraldi Woods and Schultz, 1953 – W. Pacific, Vol. 1, p. 103

Centropyge multifasciatus (Smith and Radcliffe, 1911) – W. Pacific, Vol. 1, p. 105

Centropyge nox (Bleeker, 1853) – W. Pacific, Vol. 1, p. 107

Centropyge tibicen (Cuvier, 1831) – W. Pacific, Vol. 1, p. 108

> *Holacanthus leucopleura* Bleeker, 1853

Centropyge vroliki (Bleeker, 1853) – W. Pacific, Vol. 1, p. 109

Subgenus *Xiphipops*

Centropyge acanthops (Norman, 1922) – E. Africa, Vol. 2, p. 259

Centropyge argi Woods and Kanazawa, 1951 – W. Atlantic, Vol. 2, p. 260

Centropyge aurantonotus Burgess, 1974 – W. Atlantic, Vol. 2, p. 261

Centropyge bispinosus (Günther, 1860) – Indo-West Pacific, Vol. 1, p. 98

> *Centropyge tutuilae* Jordan and Jordan, 1922

Centropyge ferrugatus Randall and Burgess, 1972 – W. Pacific, Vol. 2, p. 263

Centropyge fisheri (Snyder, 1904) – Hawaiian Islands, Vol. 2, p. 264

Centropyge flavicauda Fraser-Brunner, 1933 – W. Pacific, Vol. 1, p. 101

> *Centropyge caudoxanthurus* Shen, 1973

Centropyge flavipectoralis Randall and Klausewitz, 1977 – Sri Lanka, Vol. 2, p. 265

Centropyge hotumatua Randall and Caldwell, 1973 – S. E. Oceania, Vol. 2, p. 266

Centropyge interruptus (Tanaka, 1918) – S. Japan, Vol. 2, p. 267

Centropyge joculator Smith-Vaniz and Randall, 1974 – Cocos-Keeling Islands and Christmas Island (Ind. Ocean), Vol. 2, p. 268

Centropyge loriculus (Günther, 1860) – W. Pacific, Vol. 1, p. 104

Centropyge multicolor Randall and Wass, 1974 –

W. Pacific, Vol. 2, p. 269

Centropyge multispinis (Playfair, 1866) – Indian Ocean and Red Sea, (also possibly Australia) Vol. 1, p. 106

Centropyge nigriocellus Woods and Schultz, 1953 – W. Pacific, Vol. 2, p. 270

Centropyge potteri Jordan and Metz, 1912 – Hawaiian Islands, Vol. 2, p. 271

Centropyge resplendens Lubbock and Sankey, 1975 – Ascension Island, Vol. 2, p. 272

Centropyge shepardi Randall and Yasuda, 1979 – Guam, Vol. 2, p. 273

Genus *Chaetodontoplus* Bleeker, 1876

Scales very small (85 or more in lateral row) and not arranged in regular series; hind margin of preorbital not free; interoperculum large without spines; lateral line terminating at end of soft dorsal; vertical fins not elongate.

Chaetodontoplus ballinae Whitley, 1959 – New South Wales, Australia, Vol. 1, p. 112

Chaetodontoplus caeruleopunctatus Yasuda and Tominaga, 1976 – Philippines, Vol. 2, p. 274

Chaetodontoplus chrysocephalus Bleeker, 1854 – Japan–Taiwan, Vol. 2, p. 275
  Chaetodontoplus cephalareticulatus Shen and Lim, 1975

Chaetodontoplus conspicillatus (Waite, 1900) – Coral Sea and Lord Howe Island, Vol. 1, p. 113

Chaetodontoplus duboulayi (Günther, 1867) – Australia, E. Indies, and Taiwan, Vol. 1, p. 114
  Holacanthus darwiniensis Saville-Kent, 1890

Chaetodontoplus melanosoma (Bleeker, 1853) – Japan, Malaysia to New Guinea, Vol. 2, p. 336 and 337
  Chaetodontoplus dimidiatus Bleeker, 1877
  ? Chaetodontoplus niger Chan, 1969

Chaetodontoplus mesoleucus (Bloch, 1787) – E. Indies and Philippines, Vol. 1, p. 117
  Chaetodon mesomelas Gmelin, 1789
  Chaetodon atratus Gray, 1854

Chaetodontoplus personifer (McCulloch, 1914) – Australia, E. Indies, and Taiwan, Vol. 1, p. 118; Vol. 2, p. 337

Chaetodontoplus septentrionalis (Schlegel, 1844) – E. Indies to Japan, Vol. 2, p. 276
  Holacanthus ronin Jordan and Fowler, 1902

Genus *Genicanthus* Swainson, 1839

Scales relatively large in regular series; lateral line terminating at end of soft dorsal; interoperculum large; teeth in jaws relatively short, their length contained about five times in eye diameter; scales on operculum in 6–8 rows; caudal fin emarginate to strongly lunate.

Genicanthus bellus Randall, 1975 – W. Pacific and E. Indian Ocean, Vol. 2, p. 277

Genicanthus caudovittatus (Günther, 1860) – Red Sea and W. Indian Ocean, Vol. 2, p. 278
  Holacanthus zebra Sauvage, 1891
  Holacanthus caudibicolor Sauvage, 1891

Genicanthus lamarck (Lacépède, 1802) – Indo-West Pacific, Vol. 1, p. 127
  Holacanthus lamarcki japonicus Schmidt, 1930
  Holacanthus chapmani Herre, 1933

Genicanthus melanospilos (Bleeker, 1857) – W. Pacific, Vol. 1, p. 128

Genicanthus personatus Randall, 1975 – Hawaiian Islands, Vol. 2, p. 280
  Genicanthus macclesfieldiensis Chan, 1965 (♀)

Genicanthus semicinctus (Waite, 1900) – Lord-Howe Island, Vol. 1, p. 129

Genicanthus semifasciatus (Kamohara, 1934) – Taiwan to S. Japan, Vol. 2, p. 281
  Holacanthus fuscosus Yasuda & Tominaga, 1970

Genicanthus spinus Randall, 1975 – Pitcairn Island and Austral Islands, Vol. 2, p. 282

Genicanthus watanabei (Yasuda and Tominaga, 1970) – W. Pacific, Vol. 1, p. 130
  Genicanthus vermiculatus Shen and Lim, 1975

Genus *Holacanthus* Lacépède, 1803

Scales relatively large in regular series; lateral line terminating at end of soft dorsal; interoperculum large; teeth in jaws relatively long, their length contained less than 2–3 times in eye diameter; scales on operculum in about 9 rows; caudal fin truncate.

Subgenus *Angelichthys*

Holacanthus africanus Cadenat, 1950 – W. Africa, Vol. 2, p. 284

Holacanthus bermudensis Jordan and Rutter, 1898 – Caribbean Sea, Vol. 2, p. 286
  Holacanthus isabelita Jordan and Rutter, 1898
  Holacanthus townsendi Nichols & Mowbray, 1914
  = (*bermudensis* x *ciliaris* Hybrid), Vol. 2, p. 291

Holacanthus ciliaris (Linnaeus, 1758) – W. Atlantic, Vol. 2, p. 288
  Chaetodon squamulosus Shaw, 1789

Chaetodon parrae Schneider, 1801
Holacanthus cornutus Desmarest, 1823
Holacanthus formosus Castelnau, 1854
Angelichthys iodocus Jordan and Rutter, 1896
? *Holacanthus lunatus* Blosser, 1909

Subgenus *Holacanthus*

Holacanthus tricolor (Bloch, 1795) – W. Atlantic, Vol. 2, p. 296

Subgenus uncertain

Holacanthus venustus Yasuda and Tominaga, 1969 – Taiwan to S. Japan, Vol. 2, p. 299

Subgenus *Plitops*

Holacanthus clarionensis Gilbert, 1890 – E. Pacific, Vol. 2, p. 292
Holacanthus limbaughi Baldwin, 1963 – Clipperton Island, Vol. 2, p. 294
Holacanthus passer Valenciennes, 1846 – E. Pacific, Vol. 2, p. 295
Holacanthus strigatus Gill, 1862

Genus *Pomacanthus* Lacépède, 1803

Scales either relatively large or small; scale focus exposed to cteni area; lateral line complete; hind margin of preorbital not free; interoperculum large, without spines; color pattern often undergoes dramatic transformation from juvenile to adult stage; vertical fins or pelvic fins usually elongate.

Subgenus *Arusetta*

Pomacanthus asfur (Forsskål, 1775) – Red Sea, Vol. 2, p. 302
Holacanthus aruset Lacépède, 1802
Arusetta asfur Fraser-Brunner, 1933

Subgenus *Euxiphipops*

Pomacanthus navarchus (Cuvier, 1831) – Indo-Australian Archipelago, Vol. 1, p. 120
Euxiphipops navarchus Fraser-Brunner, 1934
Pomacanthus sexstriatus (Cuvier, 1831) – W. Pacific, Vol. 1, p. 121
Chaetodon resimus Gray, 1854
Euxiphipops sexstriatus Fraser-Brunner, 1934
Pomacanthus xanthometopon (Bleeker, 1853) – W. Pacific, Vol. 1, p. 124
Euxiphipops xanthometopon Fraser-Brunner, 1934

Subgenus *Pomacanthodes*

Pomacanthus annularis (Bloch, 1787) – India and Sri Lanka to Solomon Islands, Vol. 1, p. 134
Chaetodon vorticosus Gray, 1854
Holacanthus pseudannularis Bleeker, 1858

*new combination synonyms used widely in the aquarium hobby

Pomacanthus chrysurus (Cuvier, 1831) – N. W. Indian Ocean, Vol. 2, p. 304
Pomacanthus imperator (Bloch, 1787) – Indo-W. Pacific, Vol. 1, p. 134
Chaetodon nicobariensis Schneider, 1801
Holacanthus geometricus Lacépède, 1804
Holacanthus bishopi Seale, 1900
Holacanthus marianus Seale, 1900
Pomacanthus maculosus (Forsskål, 1775) – Red Sea to Persian Gulf, Vol. 2, p. 306
Pomacanthus semicirculatus (Cuvier, 1831) – Indo-West Pacific, Vol. 1, p. 136
Holacanthus alternans Cuvier, 1831
Holacanthus caeruleus Cuvier, 1831
Holacanthus lepidolepis Bleeker, 1853
Holacanthus ignatius Playfair, 1867
Holacanthus poecilus Peters, 1868
Holacanthus semicircularis De Vis, 1884
Holacanthus reginae Sauvage, 1891
Holacanthus alternans var. *meleagris* Alcock, 1896
Pomacanthus striatus (Rüppell, 1835) – S. Africa to Red Sea, Vol. 2, p. 310
Holacanthus rhomboides Gilchrist and Thompson, 1908
Pomacanthus zonipectus (Gill, 1862) – E. Pacific, Vol. 2, p. 311

Subgenus *Pomacanthus*

Pomacanthus arcuatus (Linnaeus, 1758) – W. Atlantic, Vol. 2, p. 300
Chaetodon aureus Bloch, 1787
Chaetodon lutescens Bonnaterre, 1788
Pomacanthus baltcatus Cuvier, 1831
Pomacanthus cingulatus Cuvier, 1831
Pomacanthus cinquecinctus Cuvier, 1831
Chaetodon littoricola Poey, 1868
Pomacanthus paru (Bloch, 1787) – Atlantic, Vol. 2, p. 308

Genus *Pygoplites* Fraser-Brunner, 1933

Scales relatively large in regular series; lateral line terminating at end of soft dorsal; interoperculum without spines, posteriorly with a narrow branch reaching the suboperculum; preorbital convex, without spines, its hind margin not free and not serrated; scales on operculum in about 8 rows.

Pygoplites diacanthus (Boddaert, 1772) – Indo-West Pacific, Vol. 1, p. 138
Chaetodon boddaerti Gmelin, 1789
Chaetodon dux Gmelin, 1789

See Shen and Liu (1979) for further characteristics, especially with regard to internal morphology.

Phylogenetic Tree of the Family *Pomacanthidae*

(based mainly on Shen and Liu, 1979)

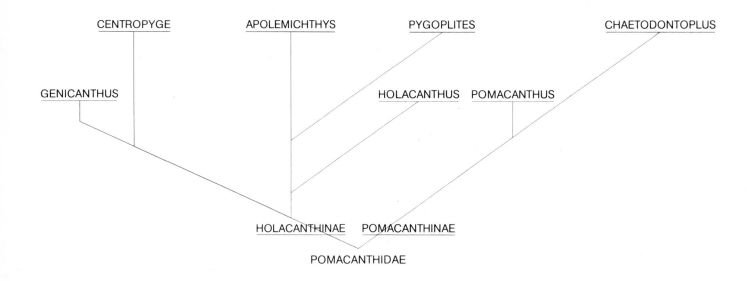

The Most Significant Characteristics in the Genera and Subgenera of the Angelfishes

Family Pomacanthidae

Genus	Subgenus	Dorsal fin	Anal fin	Vertical scale rows
Apolemichthys		XIII or XIV, 17–19	III, 17–19	about 48–50
Centropyge		XIII–XV, 15–18	III, 16–18	about 40–50
	Centropyge	XIII–XV, 15–18	III, 16–18	about 40–50
	Xiphipops	XIV–XV, 15–17	III, 16–17	about 44–50
Chaetodontoplus		XI–XIII, 16–22	III, 16–20	about 85–115
Genicanthus		XIV–XV, 16–19	III–IV, 14–19	about 45–54
Holacanthus		XIV, 17–21	III, 17–21	about 42–50
	Angelichthys	XIV, 19–21	III, 20–21	about 45–50
	Holacanthus	XIV, 17–19	III, 18–20	about 42–48
	Plitops	XIV, 17–19	III, 17–19	about 50
Pomacanthus		IX–XIV, 17–33	III, 16–24	about 46–90
	Arusetta	XI or XII, 20–22	III, 19–21	about 50
	Euxiphipops	XII–XIV, 17–20	III, 16–19	about 46–50
	Pomacanthodes	XI–XIV, 15–25	III, 18–23	about 70–90
	Pomacanthus	IX–X, 28–33	III, 22–25	about 50–90
Pygoplites		XIV, 17–19	III, 17–19	about 45–50

Genus: *Apolemichthys*

Apolemichthys arcuatus
Bandit Angelfish

(GRAY, 1831)

The Bandit Angelfish is one of several butterflyfishes and angelfishes that are known only from the Hawaiian Islands. It does not appear to be particularly common but solitary individuals are seen regularly in certain areas. It is sometimes encountered in rich coral but more often on rocky reefs, particularly where there is an abundance of ledges and caves. The species is seldom seen at depths of less than 12 meters (39 ft), in a range that extends at least to 50 meters (164 ft). Most specimens are encountered between 25 and 50 meters (82 and 164 ft). The Bandit Angelfish would have to rate as one of the most unintelligent members of the family if ease of capture with a handnet is any indication. Once sighted they are easy prey even to inexperienced aquarium fish collectors. Their natural diet consists largely of sponges and for this reason the species does not do well in captivity. Most aquarium specimens die within a few months. Juveniles are similar to adults in appearance. The maximum size is about 18 cm (7.2 in.).

348.
Apolemichthys arcuatus
Adult. Aquarium photo taken at the Taronga Zoo, Sydney.
Photo: Friese.

349.
Apolemichthys arcuatus
Adult. Underwater photo from Hawaii, at a depth of 15 m (50 ft).
Photo: Roediger.

348 ▲

349 ▼

Apolemichthys guezei
Réunion Angelfish

(RANDALL and MAUGÉ, 1978)

This species is known on the basis of only six specimens which were captured by Mr. Paul Guézé. They were taken with gill nets at depths between 60 and 80 meters (200 and 260 ft). Although presently known only from Réunion, it could be expected to occur at nearby Mauritius and possibly also Madagascar. The color pattern of this species most closely resembles that of *A. xanthopunctatus* from Oceania, but it differs significantly in having a dark head and lacking a pale-edged black spot on the nape and near the upper corner of the gill cover (these spots are also present on *A. trimaculatus*). It differs from all other species in the genus by having longer pectoral and pelvic fins (they extend to or beyond the level of the anal fin origin), and longer and more angular soft portions of the dorsal and anal fins. The maximum size is about 14 to 15 cm (5.6 to 6 in.). This species is unknown to the aquarium hobby; its maintenance is probably similar to that of *A. trimaculatus*.

350.
Apolemichthys guezei
SL 9.5 cm (3.8 in.),
TL 12 cm (4.7 in.). This recently discovered species is known only from the small island of Réunion in the Western Indian Ocean.
Photo: Randall.

Apolemichthys xanthopunctatus
Golden Spotted Angelfish

BURGESS, 1973

This species was first collected in 1954 at Kapinga-marangi Atoll, Caroline Islands, during an expedition sponsored by the George Vanderbilt Foundation. The solitary specimen was subsequently deposited at the California Academy of Sciences and was ignored for a number of years until Burgess "rediscovered" it while examining chaetodontids and pomacanthids in the CAS collection. In the meantime several specimens were collected by Dr. John Randall during a visit to the Line Islands in October 1968. *A. xanthopunctatus* is most closely related to *A. guezei* of Réunion, but unlike that species it has prominent ocelli on the nape and near the upper edge of the gill cover. A wide gap also occurs in the distribution of these species: *guezei* is known only from the western

Indian Ocean locality of Réunion, whereas *xanthopunctatus* has been found only in the Line and eastern Caroline islands, both in the central-western Pacific. This species is unknown to the aquarium hobby. The maximum size is about 25 cm (10 in.).

351.
Apolemichthys xanthopunctatus
Adult individual, SL (5.8 in.), TL 175 mm (6.9 in.).
Few specimens are known. The photo was taken at Fanning Island, which is a British protectorate; it lies about 1500 km (900 miles) south of Hawaii.
Photo: Randall.

Apolemichthys xanthotis
Red Sea Angelfish

(FRASER–BRUNNER, 1951)

352 ▲

352.
Apolemichthys xanthotis
Underwater photo from the Red Sea, at a depth of 15 m (50 ft). Photo: Roediger.

353 ▼

353.
Apolemichthys xanthotis
Underwater photo from Jeddah, Red Sea, at a depth of 8 m (26 ft). Photo: Debelius.

A Seldom Seen Group of *Apolemichthys xanthotis*

The Red Sea Angelfish is nearly identical in appearance to *A. xanthurus* from the western and central Indian Ocean. They can be differentiated easily, however, by comparing the extent of the darkened area on the head: in *xanthotis* it extends posteriorly to the level of the pelvic fins, completely engulfing the head and pectoral fin base; in *xanthurus* the dark area is restricted to the breast and that portion of the head anterior to the preopercle margin. *Apolemichthys xanthotis* is found throughout the Red Sea from the Gulf of Aqaba southward. It is also known in the adjacent Gulf of Aden. During a visit to Eilat in 1975 I occasionally encountered this species, often in pairs at depths ranging from about 10 to 25 meters (33 to 82 ft). It was usually seen in coral areas and appeared to graze on algae and possibly sponges and other benthic invertebrates. Several captive specimens, in excellent condition, were observed at the Coral World aquarium in Eilat. This species thrives in captivity. The maximum length is about 15 cm (6 in.).

354.
Apolemichthys xanthotis
A small group of this species of pygmy angelfish which is seldom observed under water. These adults have a length of about 12 cm (4.8 in.). Underwater photo from Jeddah, Red Sea, at a depth of 18 m (59 ft). Photo: Debelius.

Apolemichthys xanthurus
Indian Yellow-Tail Angelfish

(BENNETT, 1832)

355.
Apolemichthys xanthurus
Aquarium photo.
Photo: Debelius.

356.
Apolemichthys xanthurus
Nearly adult, 11 cm (4.4 in.). Underwater photo from the Maldive Islands.
Photo: Voigtmann.

355 ▲   356 ▼

This species is known from several localities in the western Indian Ocean including Mauritius, Sri Lanka and the east coast of India. It is similar in appearance to *A. xanthotis* of the Red Sea and Gulf of Aden. Both species possess the same general color pattern, but in *xanthurus* the black area of the head is much reduced and significant differences in body proportions are evident; for example, in *A. xanthurus* the body and tail base are deeper, the snout is shorter, the eye larger, and there are slightly more pored scales in the lateral line (see Klausewitz and Wongratana, 1970, for further details). The Yellow-Tail Angelfish inhabits coral reef areas in which it is generally found solitary or in pairs at depths ranging from about five to 20 meters (16 to 66 ft). The maximum size is about 15 cm (6 in.). This species is well suited for the community aquarium.

Genus: *Centropyge*

Pygmy Angelfishes

Centropyge acanthops
African Pygmy Angelfish

(NORMAN, 1922)

This poorly known species is found along the East African coast from Somali southward to the vicinity of East London, South Africa and at Mauritius. It has sometimes been confused in ichthyological literature with *C. fisheri,* a Hawaiian species. They clearly differ in coloration, however. The bright orange head and back of *acanthops* in combination with a dark blue body and yellow caudal fin are characters that distinguish this species from all other *Centropyge* in the Indo-Pacific. A similar pattern is exhibited by *C. aurantonotus* of the tropical western Atlantic, but in that species the caudal and pectoral fin are blue instead of yellow, as in *acanthops.* This species inhabits areas of coral rubble at depths between eight and 40 meters (26 and 130 ft), and frequently occurs in small groups of up to about 10 indivuduals. The species is seldom available to the aquarium hobby; only occasional exports originate from Kenya. The maximum size is about 7 cm (2.8 in.).

357.
Centropyge acanthops
Adult. 7.5 cm (3 in.).
Aquarium photo.
Photo: Norman.

Centropyge argi
Cherub Pygmy Angelfish

WOODS and KANAZAWA, 1951

358 ▲   359 ▼

This species was first collected in 1908 but was not officially described and given a scientific name until 1951. It was originally believed to be rare, but since the use of SCUBA equipment has become widespread numerous sightings and specimens have been obtained. The first specimen was collected at Bermuda, but it is now known to be widely distributed in the West Indies and southern Gulf of Mexico. Böhlke and Chaplain (1968) reported that it is sometimes seen in relatively shallow water (5 to 10 meters/16 to 33 ft) among conch shell debris at Nassau Harbor in the Bahamas. The normal habitat consists of rubble areas at depths below 30 meters (100 ft). Because of its small size and hardy nature, the species is well suited for the aquarium. Vegetable foods should be offered because various algae represent an important part of the natural diet. The maximum size is about 6.5 cm (2.6 in.).

358.
Centropyge argi
Juvenile. 4 cm in length (1.6 in.).
Aquarium photo.
Photo: Norman.

359.
Centropyge argi
Adult. Underwater photo from Bon-Aire Island (The Leeward Islands).
Photo: Randall.

Centropyge aurantonotus
Flameback Pygmy Angelfish

BURGESS, 1974

This colorful angelfish was described on the basis of two specimens taken by aquarium fish collectors at Barbados and Curaçao in the West Indies. It bears a remarkable resemblance to *C. acanthops* from the east African coast but differs in the coloration of the tail fin which is yellow in *acanthops* and dark blue in *aurantonotus*. Burgess (1974) reported that the species occurs in approximately 16 to 25 meters (52 to 82 ft) off Barbados and is commonly encountered among isolated patches of staghorn coral (*Acropora cervicornis*). He mentioned further that it has been taken by trap fishermen off the island of St. Lucia at depths in excess of 200 meters (656 ft). Although this species is not readily available in the aquarium trade, it is relatively hardy and adjusts well to life in captivity. The maximum size is about 6 cm (2.4 in.).

360 ▲   361 ▼

360.
*Centropyge
aurantonotus*
Juvenile, 3 cm. (1.2 in.).
Aquarium photo.
Photo: Norman.

361.
*Centropyge
aurantonotus*
Nearly adult, 5 cm
(2 in.). Aquarium
photo.
Photo: Norman.

Centropyge colini
Colin's Pygmy Angelfish

SMITH-VANIZ and RANDALL, 1974

Centropyge colini was first encountered in March 1974 at the Cocos-Keeling Islands (northeastern Indian Ocean) by Dr. William Smith-Vaniz and Dr. Patrick Colin. It is known on the basis of only three specimens which were collected by spear on a steep submarine dropoff at depths between 50 and 75 meters (164 and 246 ft). The rock substratum contained scattered coral heads and many crevices. Smith-Vaniz and Colin found a bonanza of new angelfishes during their month-long stay at Cocos-Keeling. In a series of dives on the steep outer reef slopes they discovered three new species: *Centropyge joculator, C. colini,* and *Genicanthus bellus.* The only other pomacanthids present were *Centropyge flavissimus, C. multifasciatus,* and *Apolemichthys trimaculatus.*

C. colini appears to be restricted to the Cocos-Keeling group, which is made up of about 25 small islands that enclose a pearshaped lagoon. Colin's Angelfish does not appear to have close relatives, although it shares certain similarities with *C. multicolor* from the western Pacific; for example both species exhibit a relatively deep body and deeply incised spinous dorsal membranes. They differ greatly, however, with respect to coloration, dorsal ray counts, and head spination. *C. colini* is unknown to the aquarium hobby. The maximum size is about 7 to 8 cm (2.8 to 3.2 in.).

362.
Centropyge colini
Adult from Cocos-Keeling Island. This is one of few photos which exist of this fish.
Photo: Smith-Vaniz and Colin.

Centropyge ferrugatus
Rusty Pygmy Angelfish

RANDALL and BURGESS, 1972

This recently described species is closely related to *C. bispinosus.* It differs primarily in color pattern and caudal fin shape and lacks the series of narrow vertical bars of *bispinosus;* instead, it has many small, irregularly shaped dark spots on the sides. The caudal fin is truncate (i. e., more or less straight on the posterior margin) instead of rounded, as in *bispinosus.* So far the species is known in a relatively limited area, but additional collections will probably increase the range. The distribution extends from Tanabe Bay (about 450 km [281 miles] southwest of Tokyo) in southern Japan to the southwestern tip of Taiwan. This species is relatively common at Okinawa in the Ryukyu Islands, which lie in the middle of the range. It inhabits depths ranging between 10 and 30 meters (33 and 100 ft) and is solitary in occurrence. Relatively few specimens have been seen in the aquarium trade, but it appears to be a relatively hardy species. The maximum size is about 9 to 10 cm (3.6 to 4 in.).

363 ▲

363.
*Centropyge
ferrugatus*
9.5 cm (3.8 in.).
Aquarium photo.
Photo: Norman.

364.
*Centropyge
ferrugatus*
Adult. Aquarium
photo.
Photo: Debelius.

364 ▼

Centropyge fisheri
Fisher's Pygmy Angelfish

(SYNDER, 1904)

365.
Centropyge fisheri
7.5 cm (3 in.).
Aquarium photo taken
in a pet shop in
Hawaii.
Photo: Allen.

366.
Centropyge fisheri
Adult. Photo from the
Wilhelma Aquarium at
Stuttgart, West Ger-
many.
Photo: Kahl.

This species has been reported from widely scattered localities in the tropical Indo-Pacific, but it appears to be restricted to the Hawaiian Islands and records from other areas probably represent misidentifications; for example, most Indian Ocean records of *C. fisheri* are actually referrable to *C. acanthops*. It is closely related to *C. flavicauda* of the western Pacific. Both species are members of the subgenus *Xiphipops*, charac-terized by the presence of a pair of stout spines on the preorbital bone. Fisher's Angelfish is common in some areas of the Hawaiian Islands, usually among dead coral rubble at depths below 30 meters (100 ft). It is particularly abundant at Molokini Rock off the coast of Maui and at this locality is some-times encountered at depths of only 10 to 15 meters (33 to 49 ft). Like most deep-dwelling *Centropyge*, *C. fisheri* does well in captivity. The maximum size is about 6 cm (2.4 in.).

365 ▲   366 ▼

Centropyge flavipectoralis
Yellowfin Pygmy Angelfish

RANDALL and KLAUSEWITZ, 1977

This species is the most recently described member of the angelfish family. It was first collected by H. R. Schmidt at Sri Lanka in 1955. The specimen was donated to the Senckenberg Museum in Frankfurt and subsequently placed in its collection under the name of *C. multispinis* (see Vol. 1 for a description of this species). Between 1966 and 1972 several more specimens were obtained by the Senckenberg Museum, and it was also collected off Sri Lanka by Mr. Roger Lubbock and Dr. John Randall, who, with Dr. Wolfgang Klausewitz of the Senckenberg Museum eventually described it as a new species. It is known only at Sri Lanka and is closely related to *C. multispinis,* which is also common at Sri Lanka but occurs elsewhere in the Indian Ocean and Red Sea. The two species can be easily separated only on the basis of pectoral fin coloration. The pectorals of *C. multispinis* are more or less transparent but have some dark pigmentation on the rays. In 1975 I observed *C. flavipectoralis* at approximately three to 12 meters (10 to 39 ft) while diving off the southern tip of Sri Lanka in an area of rubble with little coral growth. It has also been collected in the vicinity of Trincomalee, on the northeast coast, at depths between three and 20 meters (10 and 66 ft). The maximum size is about 10 cm (4 in.).

367.
Centropyge flavipectoralis
SL 7.4 cm (2.9 in.); TL 9.2 cm (3.6 in.). This specimen is from Trincomalee, Sri Lanka.
Photo: Randall.

368.
Centropyge flavipectoralis
8.5 cm (3.4 in.). Aquarium photo of one of the first live specimens to reach the United States.
Photo: Norman.

367 ▲

368 ▼

Centropyge hotumatua
Hotumatua's Pygmy Angelfish

RANDALL and CALDWELL, 1973

Centropyge hotumatua was first collected in 1969 on an expedition I made to Easter Island with Dr. John Randall. It was subsequently collected by Dr. Randall at Rapa, Pitcairn group, and Raivavae in the Austral Islands (all localities are in the southeastern corner of Oceania). The species is named after Hotumatua, the legendary Polynesian chieftain who first colonized Easter Island. At this locality the species is not uncommon at depths below about 25 meters (82 ft). It has also been found at depths as shallow as 14 meters (46 ft) at Pitcairn Island and at a maximum depth of 45 meters (148 ft), also at Pitcairn. The habitat generally consists of coral or rock with numerous crevices. The species appears to be most closely related to *C. joculator* from the Cocos-Keeling

Islands (Indian Ocean). However, the two species are easily distinguished on the basis of color pattern. *C. hotumatua* is unknown to the aquarium hobby. Its geographic distribution lies well beyond the areas normally frequented by aquarium fish collectors. The maximum size is about 8 cm (3.2 in.).

369 ▼

369.
Centropyge hotumatua
Adult, SL 6.8 cm
(2.7 in.), TL 8.8 cm
(3.5 in.). This
specimen comes from
Easter Island in the
southeast Pacific.
Photo: Randall.

Centropyge interruptus
Japanese Pygmy Angelfish

(TANAKA, 1918)

Centropyge interruptus is an inhabitant of the Pacific coast of central and southern Japan. The known distribution extends from Tosa Bay on the island of Shikoku northward to the Tokyo area of Honshu. It is reported as being common around the Izu Peninsula (about 100 km/62 miles southwest of Tokyo) and also occurs throughout the Izu Islands and the more southern Bonin Group. Burgess and Axelrod (1972) and several previous authors have confused this species with *C. fisheri* of the Hawaiian Islands, but as Tominaga and Yasuda (1973) have pointed out, *C. interruptus* is a valid species, and on the basis of color pattern, is clearly distinct from *C. fisheri*. The Japanese Angelfish inhabits rocky shores at depths of about 15 to at least 60 meters (49 to 200 ft). Juveniles are characterized by the presence of a blue-edged black spot on the soft dorsal fin. Their interesting reproductive habits which involve sex reversal were recently studied by Moyer and Nakazona, and are summarized in the introductory portion of the angelfish section. This is one of the few species of *Centropyge* known to possess color differences related to sex. The opercular region of males is marked with heavy blue lines that give the head an overall blue appearance when viewed from a distance of one or two meters (3.3 to 6.6 ft). Females, by contrast have an orange opercular area flecked with small blue dots. In addition, the posterior edge of the soft dorsal and anal fins in males is black streaked with broad, irregular bright blue patches; in females this area is uniformly blue. This colorful species appears to do well in captivity but unfortunately is seldom seen outside Japan. The maximum size is about 15 cm (6 in.)

370 ▲

371 ▼

370.
Centropyge interruptus from Miyake-jima, Japan, at a depth of 12 m (39 ft). This is one of the few species of angelfishes in which the sexes can be distinguished by color. Male above and female below.
Photo: Moyer.

371.
Centropyge interruptus
The photo of this female pygmy angelfish was taken at Miyake-jima, Izu Islands, Japan.
SL 8.3 cm (3.3 in.); TL 10.8 cm (4.3 in.).
This species has been erroneously identified as *Centropyge flavicauda* by other authors.
Photo: Randall.

Centropyge joculator
Cocos Pygmy Angelfish

SMITH-VANIZ and RANDALL, 1974

372 ▲

373 ▼

372.
Centropyge joculator
6 cm (2.4 in.). From
Christmas Island (In-
dian Ocean) at a
depth of 20 m (66 ft).
The fish is being in-
spected for parasites
by the cleaner wrasse
Labroides pectoralis.
Photo: Allen.

373.
Centropyge joculator
Adult. The species
grows to a max.
length of 9 cm (3.6 in.).
Underwater photo
from Cocos-Keeling
Islands.
Photo: Colin.

This beautiful angelfish was discovered in early 1974 at the Cocos-
Keeling Islands by an expedition
from the the Philadelphia Academy
of Sciences. More recently Roger
Steene and I took it at Christmas
Island, south of Java. It was abundant at this locality, in coral and
rubble areas on the steep outer-
reef slope at depths between 15
and 70 meters (49 and 230 ft).
Occasionally it was encountered in
only 8 to 10 meters (26 to 33 ft)
adjacent to exceptionally steep
dropoffs. It is solitary in habit or
occurs in small groups of four or
five individuals. At first glance this
species greatly resembles
C. bicolor of the western Pacific
but is easily distinguished from it
on the basis of coloration, number
of dorsal spines, shape of the
caudal fin, and depth distribution.
C. bicolor (see Vol. 1, p. 95) has a
dark bar above the eyes, 15 dorsal
spines (14 in *joculator*), and a
rounded caudal fin (subtruncate to
only slightly rounded in *joculator*)
and is usually found at depths of
less than 15 meters (49 ft). *C. joculator,* by contrast, inhabits deeper
water adjacent to steep slopes.
The photographs included here are
the first of this species in its
natural habitat to be published.
C. joculator is the only member of
the genus so far reported in which
the posterior part of the dorsal and
anal fins are slightly more elongate
in males than in females. The
maximum size is about 9 cm
(3.6 in.).

Centropyge multicolor
Multicolor Pygmy Angelfish

RANDALL and WASS, 1974

I first sighted this magnificent species in June 1974 during a 50-meter (164 ft) dive on the precipitous outer reef slope at Enewetak Atoll in the Marshall Islands. I immediately recognized it as a new *Centropyge,* but was unable to collect it because my air supply was nearly exhausted. The next day however, I returned and captured a fine specimen with the anesthetic quinaldine. For a long time it had been one of my ambitions to collect and describe either a new butterflyfish or an angelfish. At last this dream had been realized – or so I thought. It suddenly dawned on me that Dr. John Randall had mentioned collecting a spectacular new *Centropyge* at Majuro Atoll (also in the Marshall group) only a few months earlier. I decided to resolve the questition at once and made a telephone call to Dr. Randall in Hawaii with the help of a local radio operator. When he answered I quickly described the colors of the fish and was assured that indeed it was the same species. Thus I lost my new species by the narrow span of only three months (Dr. Randall had collected four specimens at Majuro in April 1974). It is remarkable how a fish species remains undiscovered for centuries and then within a few months it is found independently by several people. By an odd coincidence this same fish was collected at Tahiti by a third party, Mr. Clemens Classen, an aquarium fish collector, more than two months before Dr. Randall captured his specimens at Majuro. Both Classen and I donated our fish to Dr. Randall, who eventually described it in in conjunction with Dr. Richard Wass. The species is known only from the Marshall and Society islands, but further collecting in deep water will probably reveal its presence at other localities in the central-west Pacific. The six specimens on which Randall and Wass based their description of this species were collected on steep (nearly vertical) outer reef slopes at depths between 20 and 54 meters (66 and 177 ft). The species is presently unknown in the aquarium trade. The maximum size is about 9 cm (3.5 in.).

374.
Centropyge multicolor
Adult. Underwater photo from the Marshall Islands.
Photo: Nate Bartlett.

Centropyge nigriocellus
Black-Spot Pygmy Angelfish

WOODS and SCHULTZ, 1953

This angelfish was first described on the basis of a single specimen taken at Johnston Island by Dr. Leonard Schultz in 1946. More recently it was collected by Dr. John Randall at Fanning Island in the Line group. These islands remain the only known localities. Johnston Island is situated in the central Pacific Ocean about 900 km (563 miles) south of the Hawaiian Archipelago and Fanning Island is approximately 1900 km (1188 miles) southeast of Johnston.

Further collecting efforts in the central western Pacific will probably increase the known range of this species. The preferred habitat consists of dead coral and rubble reefs at depths between about four and 15 meters (13 and 49 ft). This species has yet to be introduced to the aquarium hobby. The maximum size is about 6 cm (2.4 in.).

375.
Centropyge nigriocellus
SL 3.8 cm (1.5 in.); TL 5.0 cm (2 in.). This individual comes from Fanning Island, south of Hawaii in the Central Pacific.
Photo: Randall.

Centropyge potteri
Potter's Pygmy Angelfish

JORDAN and METZ, 1912

This species of pygmy angelfish occurs only in the Hawaiian Islands. It is found throughout the archipelago at depths below about 10 meters (33 ft) in rock, coral, and rubble areas. Like other members of the genus it is solitary in habit and never strays far from shelter. Typically, it darts from one crevice to another, exposing itself only briefly as it moves over the reef. The fish is not nearly so attractive in its native habitat as it is in aquarium surroundings. The reason for this is that its bright red coloration is inconspicuous at the depths in which the fish normally occurs. The red areas generally appear brownish or grey-green. Small juveniles (approximately 25 to 30 mm (1 to 1.2 in.) make their appearance during late spring and summer. At this time they are relatively easy to catch with a dipnet in rocky areas like Waimea Bay on the north shore of the island of Oahu. It is not uncommon to see these juveniles at depths of only five to 10 meters (16 to 33 ft). Adult specimens are common in most areas but are difficult to capture in dense coral cover. Most aquarium specimens are collected on rocky reefs, in rubble areas, or on ledges. This species is widely exported and is popular in the aquarium trade. It quickly acclimates to life in captivity and will accept feedings of dry, frozen, and live foods. It is also fond of grazing on algae which may grow on the walls of the tank. The maximum size is about 10 cm (4 in.).

376 ▲   377 ▼

378 ▼

376.
Centropyge potteri
Aquarium photo of an adult.
Photo:
Nieuwenhuizen.

377.
Centropyge potteri
8 cm (3.2 in.).
Aquarium photo.
Photo: Norman.

378.
Centropyge potteri
Adult. Underwater photo from Rabbit Island, Oahu, Hawaii, at a depth of 8 m (26 ft).
Photo: Randall.

Centropyge resplendens
Resplendent Pygmy Angelfish

LUBBOCK and SANKEY, 1975

This species was only described recently on the basis of three specimens collected at Ascension Island in 1974. Ascension is an isolated outpost located in the central Atlantic Ocean, roughly midway between South America and Africa. The Resplendent Pygmy Angelfish is closely related to *C. argi* and *C. aurantonotus,* the other two species of *Centropyge* that occur in the tropical Atlantic. As is true with most members of the genus, these species differ chiefly in color pattern. All three species have a blue body, but in *C. argi* only the head and chest are yellow (or orange) and in *C. aurantonotus* the caudal fin and dorsal margin of the caudal peduncle are dark blue and the head is entirely orange. The overall color pattern of *C. resplendens* is remarkably similar to that found in the damselfish *Glyphidodontops starcki* (Allen) from the western Pacific. This type of similarity in morphology or color pattern in two unrelated groups is known among biologists as *convergence* and is represented by many examples in the animal and plant kingdoms. The habitat of *C. resplendens* consists of rock and rubble at depths ranging between 15 and at least 40 meters (49 and 130 ft). The distribution appears to be entirely restricted to tiny Ascension Island, but it is locally common. Few specimens have been exported to Europe, but it appears to be a good aquarium species. The maximum size is about 6 cm (2.4 in.). This species spawned in the aquarium of a pet shop in New York, but the eggs did not develop. Males and females show slight color differences. The anal fin of the male has much yellow while that of the female is primarily blue.

379 ▲

380 ▼

381 ▼

379.
Centropyge resplendens
Juvenile, 3 cm (1.2 in.).
Aquarium photo.
Photo: Norman.

380.
Centropyge resplendens
Aquarium photo of a pair. Male above and female below. About 5.5 cm (2.2 in.) in length.
Photo: Norman.

381.
Centropyge resplendens
Adults. Underwater photo from Ascension Island, Atlantic Ocean, at a depth of 20 m (66 ft).
Photo: Lubbock.

Centropyge shepardi
Shepard's Pygmy Angelfish

RANDALL and YASUDA, 1979

This species was recently discovered on coral reefs in the Mariana and Ogasawara (Bonin) islands, Pacific Ocean, and was described by Dr. John E. Randall and Dr. Fujio Yasuda who named the species after its first collector, Mr. John W. Shepard.

This species most closely resembles the widely distributed *Centropyge bispinosus,* particularly with regards to color pattern, proportional measurements, and fin ray counts. It differs, however, by usually having 17 instead of 16 pectoral rays, a slightly instead of strongly rounded caudal fin, and more lightly pigmented dorsal, anal, and caudal fins. In addition, it lacks the bluish color over the head and also a blue-edged orange-red spot at the pectoral base, both typical features of *C. bispinosus.* This species has been observed at depths ranging from 10 to 56 meters (33 to 184 ft) and usually occurs solitarily or in small groups. The diet consists primarily of benthic algae.

According to Randall and Yasuda there is evidence of sex reversal in this species. A marked territoriality is exhibited by a male fish who dominates several smaller females. This harem-type social structure is evident in several other *Centropyge* and may occur in all species of the genus. The maximum size is about 12 cm (4.8 in.).

382 ▲

382.
Centropyge shepardi
The photo of this species was taken by Dr. Randall, at a depth of 22 m (72 ft).
7.5 cm (3 in.).
Photo: Randall.

383 ▼

383.
Centropyge shepardi
Juvenile. TL 2.5 cm (1 in.) Guam, an island of the Mariana Group, about 2000 km (1250 miles) east of Manila, Philippines, is a territory of the United States.
Photo: Randall.

Genus: *Chaetodontoplus*

Chaetodontoplus caeruleopunctatus   YASUDA and TOMINAGA, 1976
Blue-Spotted Angelfish

This species is poorly known and was described on the basis of a single specimen, 77 mm (3 in.) in standard length (from snout to tail base), which was imported as an aquarium fish from the Philippine Islands. It differs from the other members of *Chaetodontoplus* by its distinctive color pattern which consists of numerous small blue spots on a dark ground color. The species appears to be restricted to the Philippine Archipelago. The maximum size is about 14 cm (5.6 in.). A juvenile specimen of about 10 cm (4 in.) was recently obtained by Dr. Klausewitz of the Senckenberg Museum in West Germany. It is thriving in captivity.

384.
Chaetodontoplus caeroleopunctatus
Subadult, 10 cm (4 in.). Aquarium photo taken at the Senckenberg Institut, Frankfurt, West Germany.
Photo: Debelius.

385.
Chaetodontoplus caeroleopunctatus
Adult. Photographed at Cebu Island in the Philippines.
Photo: Lubbock.

384 ▲   385 ▼

Chaetodontoplus chrysocephalus
Orange-Faced Angelfish

BLEEKER, 1854

This species was known for many years only on the basis of the type specimen which was collected nearly 130 years ago at Java in the Indonesian Archipelago. It still remains poorly documented and relatively few specimens have been collected. Most of these have come from Japan. Shen and Lim (1975) erroneously described a specimen from Taiwan as a new species, *Chaetodontoplus cephalareticulatus.* More recently, Yasuda and Tominaga from Japan have prepared a manuscript which suggests that the *chrysocephalus* color pattern is merely a variation of *C. septentrionalis.* It is significant that no small juveniles of *chrysocephalus* have ever been found. Most specimens have been in excess of 100 mm (4 in.) standard length, with the smallest known specimen measuring 89 mm (3.6 in.) SL. It apparently grows to a maximum size of about 22 cm (8.8 in.). The distribution ranges from southern Japan to the Indonesian Archipelago which is approximately the same as for *C. septentrionalis.*

386.
Chaetodontoplus chrysocephalus
The only specimen below 10 cm (4 in.) in length that has been illustrated. It was collected at Taiwan.
SL 8.9 cm (3.6 in.).
Photo: Shen.

387.
Chaetodontoplus chrysocephalus
SL 16.9 cm (6.7 in.); TL 20 cm (8 in.).
The fish is from the southwest of Shikoku Island, southern Japan.
Photo: Randall.

386 ▲

387 ▼

Chaetodontoplus septentrionalis (TEMMINCK and SCHLEGEL, 1844)
Blue-Stripe Angelfish

This beautiful species is easily distinguished by its vivid blue stripes on an orange-brown ground color. Small juveniles, however, are mainly black, banded with yellow at the rear of the head, and have a yellow caudal fin. The characteristic blue stripes normally begin developing at a standard length (tail not included) of about 25 to 30 mm (1 to 1.2 in.). Occasional specimens exhibit a pattern of wavy, horizontal blue lines on the head, chest, and dorsal portion of the body and are otherwise brownish with yellow caudal and pectoral fins. It was mentioned in the text for *C. chrysocephalus* that these two species may be the same. It is possible that the *septentrionalis* color pattern may represent subadult and adult females whereas males gradually change to the *chrysocephalus* pattern. However, in order to confirm this possibility it is necessary to examine the gonads from a series of specimens of both species. It is also concievable that the color transformation from the *septentrionalis* to the *chrysocephalus* phase could be confirmed by aquarium observations. The geographic range of *septentrionalis* extends from Central Japan southward to the Ryukyu Islands, Taiwan, and Hong Kong. It is not an uncommon species in some coral reef areas at depths between five and 15 meters (16 and 49 ft). Like most angelfishes it is solitary in occurrence. This species is a popular aquarium fish that does well in captivity once the initial feeding problems are overcome. The maximum size is about 20 cm (8 in.).

389.
Chaetodontoplus septentrionalis
Juvenile. 4.5 cm (1.8 in.).
Aquarium photo.
Photo: Shen.

391 ▼

390.
Chaetodontoplus septentrionalis
9 cm (3.5 in.).
Aquarium photo.
Photo: Norman.

391.
Chaetodontoplus septentrionalis
Adult. 18 cm (7.2 in.).
Aquarium photo.
Photo: Friese.

389 ▲   390 ▼

Genus: *Genicanthus*

Genicanthus bellus
Ornate Angelfish

RANDALL, 1975

This species is perhaps the most spectacularly marked of all the *Genicanthus* angelfishes. Unlike most members of the genus, both males and females have a striking color pattern. The species has an unusual geographic distribution; it is known only around Tahiti in the Pacific Ocean and the Cocos-Keeling Islands in the eastern Indian Ocean. It may occur at intermediate localities but so far has eluded collectors because of its deep dwelling habits. Only a small number of specimens have been collected. All were taken from outer reef habitats adjacent to steep dropoffs at depths between 50 and 75 meters (164 and 246 ft). It generally occurs in aggregations that swim five to six meters (16 to 20 ft) out from the slope but quickly retreat to the

protective shelter of the reef when approached by a diver. Except for rare imports from Tahiti, this species is seldom seen in the aquarium trade. It always commands a high price and makes a good aquarium fish. The maximum size is about 17 cm (6.8 in.).

392.
Genicanthus bellus, male. Cocos-Keeling Islands. Photo: Smith-Vaniz and Colin.

393.
Genicanthus bellus Adult female from the Cocos-Keeling Islands. Photo: Smith-Vaniz and Colin.

394.
Genicanthus bellus, male. SL 9.7 cm (3.8 in.); TL 14 cm (5.5 in.). From Tahiti. Photo: Randall.

395.
Genicanthus bellus female. SL 10.2 cm (4 in.); TL 18.5 cm (7.4 in.). From Tahiti, at a depth of 70 m (230 ft). Photo: Randall.

392 ▼

393 ▼

394 ▼

395 ▼

Genicanthus caudovittatus
Zebra Angelfish

(GÜNTHER, 1860)

396 ▲

The Zebra Angelfish is similar in appearance to *G. melanospilos* (see Vol. 1) from the western Pacific. The male of *caudovittatus,* however, has more bars on the sides and exhibits a broad blackish area that covers much of the spinous dorsal fin; females of the two species show more similarities than males, but that of *caudovittatus* is distinguished by a dark bar above the eye. This species occurs in the Red Sea, at Mauritius, and along the east coast of Africa. It appears to be rare in the latter region and has been recorded only at Malindi, Kenya, and Pinda, Mozambique. The sparse representation of this species from East Africa, however, probably reflects the absence of deep reef collecting. In the Red Sea it is relatively common in the Gulf of Aqaba at depths between about 25 and 50 meters (82 and 164 ft). A single male is usually seen with several females, commonly on steep slopes. The males in particular are conspicuous from a considerable distance. Aggregations of these fish swim up to several meters above the bottom in search of planktonic food. Small specimens in the female color phase are relatively hardy and make good aquarium fish. The maximun size is about 20 cm (8 in.).

397 ▼

398 ▼

396.
This rare underwater photo shows an animal during sex reversal. Gulf of Aqaba, Red Sea, at a depth of 12 m (39 ft).
Photo: Debelius.

397.
Genicanthus caudovittatus
Adult female, about 12 cm (4.8 in.) in length. Gulf of Aqaba, Red Sea. Underwater photo at a depth of 12 m (39 ft).
Photo: Debelius.

398.
Genicanthus caudovittatus
Male. Underwater photo from the Red Sea, at a depth of 20 m (66 ft).
Photo: Roediger.

Genicanthus caudovittatus on the Reef

399.
A small group of
Genicanthus caudovittatus, Gulf of Aqaba.
Photo: Debelius.

399 ▲   400 ▼

400.
This underwater photo
shows a pair of *Genicanthus caudovittatus*
during courtship. The
much larger male and
the smaller female
can be distinguished
clearly by color pattern.
Photo: Debelius.

Genicanthus personatus
Masked Angelfish

RANDALL, 1975

401 ▲

402 ▼

This species was originally described on the basis of four female specimens taken off the islands of Hawaii and Oahu by aquarium fish collectors in 1972 and 1973. In the description Randall predicted that the male form (still unknown at that time) would be different from the female and would probably be characterized by a series of dark bars on the side. Finally in October 1975 two males were taken with a bottom trawl by the research vessel *Townsend Cromwell* in the vicinity of Nihoa Island, Leeward Hawaiian Islands. Dr. Randall's prediction was only half correct. Indeed, the male was different, but it completely lacked bars. Instead the head and fins were rimmed with a beautiful yellow-orange. The species is known only in the Hawaiian Islands and appears to be rare. Its normal habitat, however, probably lies below depths usually penetrated by divers. The eight known specimens reported by Randall (1975) and Randall and Struhsaker (1976) were captured at depths between 23 and 84 meters (75 and 275 ft). Randall and Struhsaker reported that the stomach of one of the male specimens was filled with the green alga *Codium,* a few shrimp larvae, and some fish eggs. Apparently it is not a good aquarium fish. One specimen was kept alive in an aquarium for two months but refused to accept food. The maximum size is about 21 cm (8.4 in.).

401.
*Genicanthus
personatus*
Female SL 9.3 cm
(3.7 in.); TL 11.5 cm
(4.5 in.). Oahu, Hawaii,
from a depth of 25 m
(82 ft).
Photo: Randall.

402.
*Genicanthus
personatus*
Male SL 15.5 cm
(6 in.); TL 22.6 cm
(9 in.). Hawaiian Is-
lands.
Photo: Randall.

Genicanthus semifasciatus
Japanese Swallow

(KAMOHARA, 1934)

This species occurs off southern Japan, the Ryukyu Islands, Taiwan, and the northern Philippines. In Japan it is generally rare except around the Izu Islands, where it inhabits rocky areas. The depth range extends from about 15 to at least 100 meters (50 to 330 ft). The distinctly colored female was described as a separate species, *Holacanthus fuscosus,* by Yasuda and Tominaga on the basis of a single specimen from Miyake Island (approximately 170 km south of Tokyo). Although there appear to be no published observation records of the two color forms occurring together, Randall (1975) deduced that *fuscosus* was probably the female of *semifasciatus* and this opinion was eventually substantiated by Shen and Liu (1976), who described female to male sex inversion in aquarium specimens. The sex change generally occurs at standard lengths between 80 and 110 mm (3.2 and 4.4 in.). Smaller fish (i. e., below 80 mm [3.2 in.] SL) which exhibit the *fuscosus* color phase, are females or immature. There are little aquarium data available for this species, but it appears to be hardy. It requires standard food such as chopped beef, freezedried shrimp, mysis, etc. The maximum size is about 21 cm (8.4 in.).

403 ▲   404 ▼

405 ▼

403.
Genicanthus semifasciatus
Female (formerly known as G. fuscosus). Underwater photo, southern Japan.
Photo: Yasuda.

404.
Genicanthus semifasciatus
The animal is shown during sex transformation from female to male. The head bar of the female is still visible, while it has disappeared in the animal shown in the photo below.
Photo: Norman.

405.
Genicanthus semifasciatus
Male, SL 10.5 cm (4 in.). Taiwan.
Photo: Shen.

Genicanthus spinus
Pitcairn Angelfish

RANDALL, 1975

406 ▲   407 ▼

This species was first collected in early 1975 by Dr. John Randall during a visit sponsored by the National Geographic Society to remote Pitcairn Island. It is most closely related to *G. semicinctus* (see Vol. 1) from Lord Howe Island but differs primarily in coloration (both male and female). Most of the known specimens were procured at Pitcairn Island, but it was also seen by Randall at Raivavae and Rurutu in the Austral Islands and at Ducie Atoll (Pitcairn group) which is the easternmost and southernmost atoll in Oceania (24°40'S, 124°47'W). This species inhabits rock and coral reef at depths ranging from about 30 to at least 60 meters (100 – 200 ft). It generally forms aggregations that swim high above the bottom. Their diet consists largely of zooplankton, although some benthic material is probably consumed. Aquarium imports of this species are unknown. The maximum size is about 35 cm (14 in.), including the elongate tail filaments.

406.
Genicanthus spinus
Female, SL 16.5 cm
(6.5 in.); TL 25 cm
(10 in.). Pitcairn.
Photo: Randall.

407.
Genicanthus spinus
Male, SL 20.6 cm
(8 in.); TL 37 cm
(14.8 in.). Pitcairn.
Photo: Randall.

Genus
Holacanthus

408.
Holacanthus tricolor
Underwater photo
taken at Mona Island,
Caribbean Sea.
Photo: Allen.

Holacanthus africanus
West African Angelfish

CADENAT, 1950

409 ▲

410 ▼

This angelfish is distributed along the tropical coast of West Africa between Senegal and the Congo. It is moderately common off Ghana where it is generally found among rocks. The species has a relatively broad depth distribution which extends from about one or two meters (3.3 to 6.6 ft) to at least 40 meters (130 ft). Like many other angelfishes, this species undergoes a dramatic color transition related to growth. Juveniles are characterized by a bright orange tail and an orange border on the dorsal fin. In addition, there is a prominent white band across the middle of the body. These markings gradually fade with growth and the pattern of adults is comparatively drab. Few marine aquarium fishes are imported from the West African region; therefore this angelfish is seldom seen in captivity. The maximum size is about 45 cm (18 in.).

411 ▼

409.
Holacanthus africanus
Juvenile from the
Ghana coast.
Photo: Lubbock.

410.
Holacanthus africanus
Juvenile, SL 5 cm
(2 in.). Ghana.
Photo: Lubbock.

411.
Holacanthus africanus
Subadult, 11 cm
(4.4 in.). Underwater
photo from the Cape
Verde Islands.
Photo: Debelius.

412.
Holacanthus africanus
Adult, 15 cm (6 in.).
Underwater photo
from the Cape Verde
Islands.
Photo: Debelius.

412 ▲   413 ▼

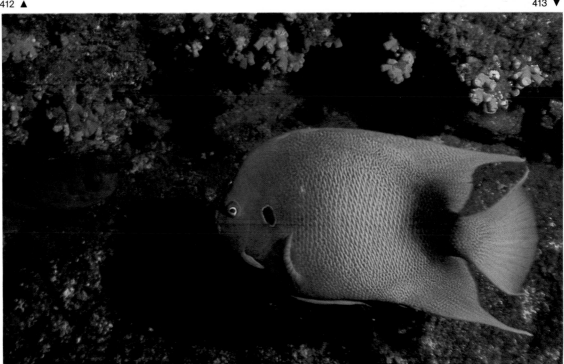

413.
Holacanthus africanus
Adult, 22 cm (8.8 in.).
Cape Verde Islands.
Photo: Debelius.

Holacanthus bermudensis
Blue Angelfish

JORDAN and RUTTER, 1898

This species is closely related to the Queen Angelfish *(H. ciliaris)* but differs primarily in color pattern. It is distributed in the Gulf of Mexico, off southern Florida, Bermuda, and the Bahamas. The depth range extends from shallow water to at least 60 meters (200 ft). It occasionally interbreeds with the Queen Angel and naturally occurring hybrids of these two species are not uncommon. The description of *Holacanthus townsendi* was based on a hybrid cross of this type. Small juveniles of the Blue Angel make fine aquarium pets once they begin to accept food. The maximum size is about 45 cm (18 in.). For more information, see *H. ciliaris*, p. 288.

414 ▲   415 ▼

Holacanthus bermudensis

414.
Holacanthus bermudensis
Juvenile, 5.5 cm
(2.2 in.). Aquarium
photo.
Photo: Norman.

415.
Holacanthus bermudensis
Adult, 22 cm (8.8 in.).
Aquarium photo.
Photo: Norman.

416.
Holacanthus bermudensis
Juvenile undergoing
color transformation
at a length of about
10 cm (4 in.).
Aquarium photo.
Photo:
Nieuwenhuizen.

Holacanthus ciliaris
Queen Angelfish

(LINNAEUS, 1758)

417 ▲   418 ▼

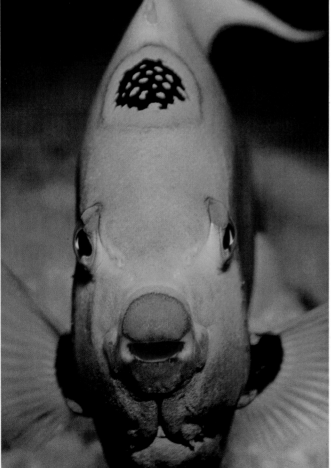

The beautiful Queen Angelfish is well known to European and American aquarists. It is an inhabitant of western Atlantic coral reefs ranging from Brazil northward to Florida, the Bahamas, and the Gulf of Mexico. It is generally solitary or found in pairs in shallow water down to at least 70 meters (230 ft). Randall (1967) examined the stomach contents of 26 specimens and reported that the species feeds almost exclusively on sponges supplemented by small amounts of algae, tunicates, hydroids, and bryozoans. A wide variety of sponges is eaten. Randall and Hartman (1968) listed 40 sponge species belonging to nearly the same number of genera among the gut contents. Juveniles occasionally remove ectoparasites from other fishes. The maximum size is about 45 cm (18 in.). This species is one of the hardiest angelfishes for the aquarium. The food should be enriched with vitamins at regular intervals.

417.
Holacanthus ciliaris
Juvenile, 5 cm (2 in.).
Underwater photo
from the Bahamas.
Photo: Hackmann.

418.
Portrait of
Holacanthus ciliaris.
Aquarium photo.
Photo: Kahl.

419.
Holacanthus ciliaris
in a 2000-liter
(440 gal.) tank of
Klaus Jungbluth, West
Germany. Adult about
30 cm (12 in.) in length.
Photo: Baensch.

Holacanthus ciliaris

Color Variations of *Holacanthus ciliaris*

420 ▲   421 ▼

422 ▼

423 ▲   424 ▼

Hybrid of *Holacanthus ciliaris* x *Holacanthus bermudensis*

420.
Holacanthus ciliaris
Juvenile, 10 cm (4 in.).
Blue phase.
Photo: Norman.

421.
Holacanthus ciliaris
Juvenile. Yellow
phase.
Photo: Friese.

422.
Holacanthus ciliaris
Juvenile, 8 cm (3 in.).
Green phase.
Photo: Norman.

423.
Holacanthus ciliaris
Adult, Yellow phase.
Underwater photo
from the Bahama
Islands.
Photo: Yanowitz.

424.
Holacanthus ciliaris
Adult, 38 cm (15 in.).
Green phase. Under-
water photo from Ro-
se Island, New
Providence, Bahamas.
At a depth of 2 m
(6.6 ft).
Photo: Baensch.

425 ▲   426 ▼

425.
Holacanthus ciliaris x
*Holacanthus
bermudensis hybrid.*
Juvenile, 8.5 cm
(3.4 in.). Aquarium
photo.
Photo: Norman.

426.
Holacanthus ciliaris x
*Holacanthus
bermudensis hybrid.*
Subadult, about
18 cm (7 in.).
Aquarium photo taken
at the Taronga Zoo,
Sydney.
Photo: Friese.

Holacanthus clarionensis
Clarion Angelfish

GILBERT, 1890

427 ▲

The Clarion Angelfish is found in the eastern tropical Pacific but evidently has a relatively limited distribution. It is known primarily from various islands and island groups that lie well off the coast of Mexico in a range that includes Clipperton Island and the Revillagigedos Group and nearby Clarion Island. The species is reported to be common around these areas. It has also been found in the vicinity of Cape San Lucas at the tip of Baja California but is apparently rare. The species is closely related to the King Angelfish *H. passer* and the juveniles of these two species are virtually identical. Although rarely seen in Europe, the Clarion Angelfish is frequently available to American hobbyists. The species is hardy in captivity, but because of its aggressive nature more than one

428 ▼

individual should not be kept in the same tank. The maximum size is about 20 cm (8 in.).

429.
Holacanthus clarionensis
Adult. Taronga Aquarium, Sydney.
Photo: Friese.

430.
Holacanthus clarionensis
A school feeding on a Mexican coral reef.
Photo: Powell.

428.
Holacanthus clarionensis
Subadult. Underwater photo from the Pacific coast of Mexico.
Photo: Powell.

427.
Holacanthus clarionensis
Juvenile, 5 cm (2 in.).
Aquarium photo.
Photo: Friese.

429 ▲   430 ▼

Holacanthus limbaughi
Clipperton Angelfish

BALDWIN, 1963

This species was first collected during two expeditions to Clipperton Island by the Scripps Institution of Oceanography in 1956 and 1958. It has not been found at any other locality. Clipperton is a remote coral atoll that lies approximately 2560 km (1600 miles) due west of Costa Rica in the tropical eastern Pacific. The 11 specimens that form the basis of the original description were taken a short distance from shore with explosives, spears, and a handnet. Baldwin (1963) reported that the species appears to be fairly common close to shore in about six to 10 meters (20 to 33 ft) but its range apparently extends into deeper water. Juveniles, which are similar to *H. passer* and *H. clarionensis* in color pattern, exhibit a series of seven narrow vertical bars on the head and body. The maximum length is about 25 cm (10 in.).

431.
Painting of *Holacanthus limbaughi*. Unfortunately no photo exists of this rare species from Clipperton Island in the eastern Pacific Ocean.
Painting: Thompson.

Holacanthus passer
King Angelfish

VALENCIENNES, 1846

This species was originally described from the Galápagos Islands, but is now known to range widely along the west coast of tropical America as far north as the Gulf of California. It is found in rocky areas in which the water is generally clear. It appears to be restricted to the central and southern portions of the Gulf at depths ranging from only a few to at least 80 meters (260 ft). The bright colored juveniles usually hide in dark crevices of the reef and seldom leave their shelter. Adults are relatively common in the Gulf, but are extremely wary and difficult to approach at close range. Young specimens are found in the Gulf of California during the winter months and are excellent aquarium fish. However, they are territorial and aggressive toward their own kind and for this reason only one King Angelfish is recommended per tank. The natural diet of this species consists of sponges, tunicates, and other benthic invertebrates. The maximum size is about 25 cm (10 in.).

432. ▲   433. ▼

432.
Holacanthus passer
Juvenile, 4.5 cm (1.8 in.). Underwater photo from Baja California. The coloration of a more advanced juvenile is shown on the jacket, top left. Photo: Hall.

433.
Holacanthus passer
Adult. Underwater photo from Baja California.
Photo: Debelius.

Holacanthus tricolor
Rock Beauty

(BLOCH, 1795)

This species is the most common angelfish on the
coral reefs of the tropical western Atlantic. Juveniles
are primarily bright yellow with a small blue-edged
black spot on the upper back and at first glance
somewhat resemble the damselfish *Stegastes
planifrons.* With growth the dark spot gradually
expands until most of the posterior two-thirds of the
fish is covered with dark pigmentation. The species
is found in a variety of habitats which includes rock
jetties, rubble reefs, and rich coral areas at depths
ranging from one meter (3.3 ft) or less for juveniles
to 30 meters (100 ft) or more. At Mona Island,
situated halfway between Puerto Rico and the Domi-
nican Republic, I found the adults common at
5 to 18 meters (16 to 59 ft). Young specimens are
well suited to aquarium conditions and will thrive in
captivity but like most angelfishes are prone to fighting among themselves. Therefore more than one
specimen per community tank is not recommended.
Their natural diet consists largely of tunicates,
sponges, zoantharians, and algae. The maximum size
is about 30 cm (12 in.).

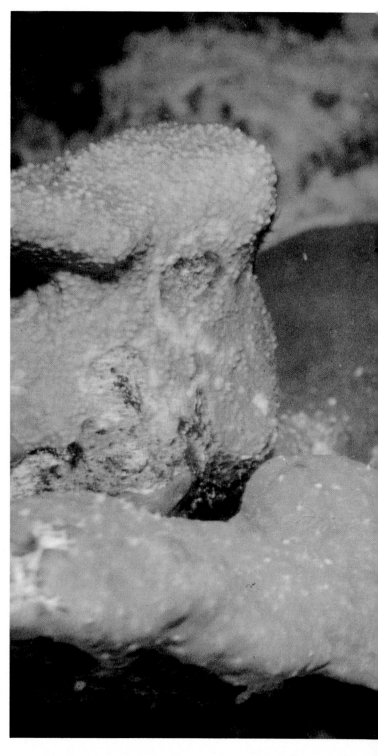

434.
Holacanthus tricolor
Adult. Underwater
photo from New Provi-
dence, Bahama Is-
lands, at a depth of
5 m (16.4 ft).
Photo: Baensch.

Holacanthus tricolor, Juvenile Stage

435 ▲

436 ▲

435.
Holacanthus tricolor
Juvenile, 3 cm (1.2 in.).
Underwater photo,
Bahama Islands.
Photo: Baensch.

436.
The damselfish
Stegastes planifrons
looks similar to the
young of *H. tricolor.*
Underwater photo,

New Providence,
Bahama Islands, at a
depth of 5 m (16.4 ft).
Photo: Baensch.

437.
Holacanthus tricolor
6 cm (2.4 in.).
Aquarium photo.
Photo: Kahl.

438.
Holacanthus tricolor
10 cm (4 in.).
Aquarium photo.
Photo: Norman.

437 ▼

438 ▼

Holacanthus venustus
Purple-Mask Angelfish

YASUDA and TOMINAGA, 1969

This species was first discovered at Ishigaki Island in the Ryukyu Group in 1967 but initial efforts to collect it were unsuccessful. It was subsequently taken in 1969 at Oshima (about 100 km/60 miles south of Tokyo) in the Izu Islands. Since that time numerous specimens have been procured and observations made from southern Japan southward to Taiwan. In 1976 I had the opportunity to observe this beautiful angelfish in its natural habitat at Sesoko Island, Okinawa. Several solitary individuals were sighted on the steep outer reef slope at depths between 15 and 35 meters (49 and 115 ft). It appeared to be a shy and retiring fish, not easily approached at close range. Apparently it is seldom available in the aquarium trade, but it would certainly make a welcome addition to any marine tank. Juvenile specimens are similar to adults in coloration. The maximum size is about 10 cm (4 in.).

439 ▲

439.
Holacanthus venustus
SL 8.6 cm (3.4 in.);
TL 11 cm (4.4 in.). The photo was taken at Sesoko Island, Okinawa, Japan. Adults of this species resemble the genus *Centropyge*.
Photo: Randall.

440 ▼

440.
Holacanthus venustus
Adult, 10 cm (4 in.)
Underwater photo, southern Japan.
Photo: Yasuda.

Genus: *Pomacanthus*

Pomacanthus arcuatus
Grey Angelfish

(LINNAEUS, 1758)

441.
Pomacanthus arcuatus
Juvenile, 6 cm
(2.4 in.). Aquarium
photo.
Photo: Norman.

441 ▲   442 ▼

The Grey Angelfish is an inhabitant
of the tropical western Atlantic; it
ranges from the vicinity of Rio de
Janeiro northward to Florida and
occasionally to the New England
region. It is relatively common in
coral reef areas, usually alone or
sometimes in pairs at depths of
only a few to at least 30 meters
(100 ft). Adult specimens are large
and form a conspicuous part of
the reef fauna. They are typically
unafraid of divers and can be
approached at close range. Randall
(1967) reported sponges as the
dominant dietary item, with lesser
amounts of tunicates, algae, zoantharians, gorgonians, hydroids,
bryozoans, and seagrasses being
ingested. The adults are too large
for the average home aquarium,
but the colorful juveniles make
fine pets. The maximum size is
about 50 cm (20 in.). Juveniles of
10 to 15 cm (4 to 6 in.) sometimes
live for several years in captivity.

442.
Pomacanthus arcuatus
Subadult, 22 cm
(8.8 in.). Underwater
photo, New Provi-
dence, at a depth of
3 m (10 ft).
Photo: Baensch.

443.
Pomacanthus arcuatus
Adult pair. Under-
water photo from the
Bahama Islands.
Photo: Roediger.

Pomacanthus arcuatus with the Sea Fan
Gorgonia ventalina

Pomacanthus asfur
Arabian Angelfish

(FORSSKÅL, 1775)

The Arabian Angelfish is an inhabitant of the Red Sea and the adjacent Gulf of Aden. During a 1977 trip to Jeddah on the Arabian side of the central Red Sea I found this species to be moderately common around semi-protected inshore reefs characterized by rich soft and hard coral growth, occasional patches of silt bottom, and frequently reduced visibility (compared with that of more offshore reefs). It is a shy species but, with patience, can eventually be approached and photographed at close range. It is usually seen around caves and in crevices, but occasionally for brief periods it comes out into the open. The depth range around Jeddah extended from about three to 15 meters (10 to 49 ft). The juvenile stage is typical for the genus and similar to that of *P. maculosus* which also occurs in the Red Sea. The tail of *asfur,* however, is yellow instead of white as in *maculosus,* and small juveniles usually have a streak of yellow extending from the middle of the sides onto the soft dorsal fin. The maximum size is about 40 cm (16 in.). This species seldom grows more than 24 cm (9.6 in.) in length in captivity. It is very aggressive towards its own species, unless

444 ▲

445 ▼

444.
Pomacanthus asfur
Juvenile from the "Three Brothers" Islands off Djibouti, Gulf of Aden.
Photo: Randall.

445.
Pomacanthus asfur
Juvenile, about 10 cm (4 in.) undergoing color transformation.
Aquarium photo.
Photo: Kahl.

Pomacanthus asfur on the Reef

paired. Small specimens will thrive in a tank of
300 liters (80 U.S. gal.), but require sufficient
hiding places.

446.
Pomacanthus asfur
Adult, 25 cm (10 in.)
Jeddah, Red Sea, at a
depth of 6 m (20 ft).
Photo: Allen.

Pomacanthus chrysurus
Ear-Spot Angelfish

(CUVIER, 1831)

447.
*Pomacanthus
chrysurus*
Juvenile, 8 cm (3 in.).
Aquarium photo.
Photo: Norman.

448a.
*Pomacanthus
chrysurus*
Adult. Underwater
photo from Kenya.
Photo: Langhoff.

The common name of this species is derived from the orange-ringed, black marking on the rear portion of the head near the beginning of the lateral line. This feature is not evident on the juveniles but gradually develops with growth. The distribution of this species is not well documented, but it appears to be widespread in the northwestern Indian Ocean. It has also been reported in the Seychelles and along the African coast from Zanzibar to the Gulf of Aden. This species is seldom seen in the aquarium trade and consequently there is little information regarding its care and maintenance in captivity. The maximum size is about 25 cm (10 in.).

447 ▲

448a ▼

448b.
*Pomacanthus
chrysurus*
12 cm (4.8 in.).
Aquarium photo.
Photo: Debelius.

448b ▼

Pomacanthus chrysurus x *P. maculosus*

449.
This fish probably represents a hybrid cross between *Pomacanthus chrysurus* and *P. maculosus*. The photo was taken at Malindi, Kenya. The color pattern is a compromise between that of the two presumed parents. The anal fin has the colouring of *P. maculosus*, but the caudal is bright yellow as in *P. chrysurus*. The curved yellow bars on the sides are also inherited from the *chrysurus* parent, but close examination reveals the presence of dusky scale margins on the anterior half of the body, a typical feature of *maculosus*. The head coloration is also similar to *maculosus* and the fish lacks the bright yellow ring on the upper portion of the gill cover which is found in *chrysurus*. In addition, the anal fin shape represents a compromise between the presumed parents. It is intermediate in shape between the rounded fin of *chrysurus* and the very pointed and elongate fin of *maculosus*. Photo: Roediger.

▼ 449

Pomacanthus maculosus
Yellow-Band Angelfish

(FORSSKÅL, 1775)

This attractive species is found in the vicinity of the Arabian Peninsula. It occurs in the Persian Gulf, the northwestern Indian Ocean, and throughout the Red Sea. From personal diving experience in these areas it seems to be most abundant in the Gulf of Oman, particularly near Muscat. The few specimens seen in the Red Sea at Eilat and Jeddah were generally encountered in silty harbors and embayments in the vicinity of coral reefs and wreckage. At Muscat many solitary individuals

were met on each dive. The habitat at Muscat consisted primarily of rich coral areas in depths between about four and 12 meters (13 and 39 ft). This fish is extremely curious and will often approach a diver within a meter or so. After an initial contact, however, it frequently retreats into the shelter of the reef, emerging periodically to have another look. Its bold color pattern and curious nature make it a prime target for underwater photographers. At Bahrain and Qatar in the Persian Gulf this

450 ▲   451 ▼

450.
Pomacanthus maculosus
Juvenile. Underwater photo from Doha, Qatar, Persian Gulf, at a depth of 3 m (10 ft). Photo: Allen.

451.
Pomacanthus maculosus
Subadult. Photo taken at the Taronga Aquarium, Sydney. Photo: Friese.

species is considered good eating and large adults are often sold in the local fish markets. It seems a shame to kill and eat something so beautiful! Juvenile specimens have a series of narrow white bars and undergo a dramatic color transition at a size of about 10 to 15 cm (4 to 6 in.). Small specimens are well suited to life in captivity and will live a long time in aquarium surroundings if properly cared for. The adults, which reach a maximum size of about 30 cm (12 in.), are much too large for the average home aquarium.

452.
Pomacanthus maculosus
Adult. Underwater night photo, Red Sea.
Photo: Schuch.

Pomacanthus paru
French Angelfish

(BLOCH, 1787)

453 ▲

This is one of the large angelfish species that inhabit coral reefs of the tropical Atlantic. It is similar in overall appearance to the Grey Angelfish but has a much darker ground color and narrow yellow or whitish scale margins. The juveniles of these two species are even more alike than the adults and are best differentiated on the basis of caudal fin coloration: in *paru* the caudal is rounded and there is a relatively narrow, pale margin around the dark area in the center of the fin; the tail fin of the Grey Angel *(P. arcuatus)* by contrast is truncated and has a broader pale margin. Randall (1967) examined the stomach contents of 23 specimens of the French Angelfish and found mainly sponges and algae and lesser amounts of zoantharians, tunicates, gorgonians, hydroids, bryozoans, spermatophytes, and unidentified eggs. The juveniles obtain part of their nourishment by feeding on ectoparasites which they remove from other fishes in the same manner as the cleaner wrasses *(Labroides)*. This species has been reported in West Africa as well as the western Atlantic, in which area it is known from Brazil northward to the Bahamas and Florida. Juveniles are well suited to aquarium life, although very small individuals (under about 12 cm/4.8 in.). are sometimes difficult to maintain. The maximum size is about 38 cm (15 in.).

453.
Pomacanthus paru
Juvenile, 7 cm (2.8 in.).
Underwater photo.
Photo: Hackmann.

454.
Pomacanthus paru
15 cm (6 in.).
Aquarium photo.
Photo: Norman.

454 ▼

455 ▼

455.
Pomacanthus paru
Juvenile, 5 cm (2 in.).
Aquarium photo.
Photo: Norman.

456.
Pomacanthus paru
Adult. Underwater photo. Bahama Islands.
Photo: Schott.

A Beautiful Specimen of *Pomacanthus paru,* Caribbean Sea

Pomacanthus striatus
Old Woman Angelfish

(RÜPPELL, 1835)

457 ▲

458 ▼

Compared with other members of the genus *Pomacanthus,* the adults of this species have a very uncharacteristic body shape and coloration. Large specimens posses a pronounced hump on the forehead and a gradually sloping, angular dorsal profile. Because of these features it is not likely to be confused with other angelfishes. Juveniles have a more typical *Pomacanthus* color pattern which consists of narrow white bars on a dark blue ground. Apparently the species is restricted to the East African coast and offshore islands, including Madagascar. The known range extends from the southern Red Sea to Knysna, South Africa (about 450 km [281 miles] east of Cape Town). According to Smith (1949), it is not uncommon at Delagoa Bay, Mozambique. Adults are too large for most aquaria, but the brightly patterned juveniles make handsome pets. The maximum size is about 46 cm (18.4 in.). The flesh is said to be good eating.

457.
Pomacanthus striatus
Juvenile, 6 cm TL
(2.4 in.). Underwater
photo from Sodwana
Bay, South Africa.
Photo: Allen.

458.
Pomacanthus striatus
SL 26.4 cm (10.6 in.);
TL 32.6 cm (13 in.).
Coast of Natal, from a
depth of 12 m (39 ft).
Photo: Randall.

Pomacanthus zonipectus
Cortez Angelfish

(GILL, 1862)

The Cortez Angelfish is an inhabitant of rock and coral reefs in the eastern tropical Pacific from the Gulf of California southward to Columbia. Alex Kerstitch of the University of Arizona is currently involved in studies of fishes in the Gulf of California and recently published (Kerstitch, 1977) these remarks about *P. zonipectus:* "Like the barberfish *(Chaetodon nigrirostris),* the juvenile Cortez angelfish is an active symbiotic cleaner of larger fish, but there is no evidence that the adult retains this cleaning behavior. The diet of this angelfish consists mostly of colonial tunicates and sponges. It also feeds occasionally on algae, hydroids, bryozoans, and fish eggs. Both adults and juveniles are typically patch reef residents in areas that are predominantly sandy with rocky outcroppings. This pomacanthid is normally found in depths of between six to 12 meters (20 to 40 ft), but has been observed as deep as 33 meters (108 ft). Occasionally, it is captured by shrimpers in their otter trawls which indicates this species' preference for sandy bottoms."

Kerstitch also mentions that the juveniles are strongly territorial and even battle among themselves in a bucket when freshly captured. The adults are quite fearless and frequently approach divers at close range. Young specimens make good aquarium pets and are suitable for a community tank as long as no conspecifics are present. The maximum size is about 46 cm (18.4 in.). The species is sensitive to lymphocystis and therefore needs extremely good water conditions.

459 ▲   460 ▼

459.
Pomacanthus zonipectus
Juvenile, Perlas Islands, Pacific coast of Panama. Underwater photo taken at a depth of 5 m (16 ft). Photo: Roediger.

460.
Pomacanthus zonipectus
Adult, 28 cm (11 in.). Perlas Islands at a depth of 5 m (16 ft). Photo: Roediger.

Index Chart
of the Juveniles of the Genera *Holacanthus* and *Pomacanthus*

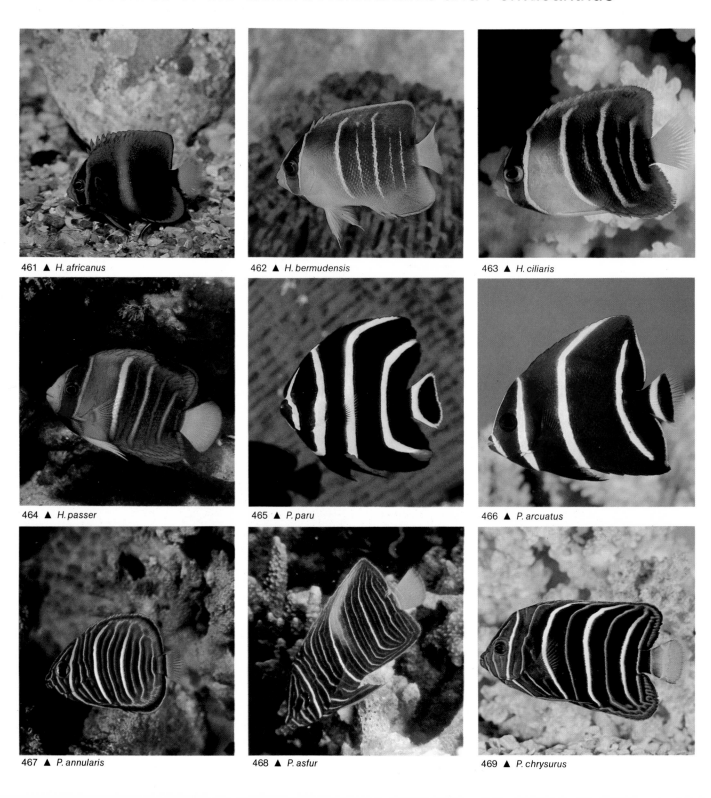

461 ▲ *H. africanus*

462 ▲ *H. bermudensis*

463 ▲ *H. ciliaris*

464 ▲ *H. passer*

465 ▲ *P. paru*

466 ▲ *P. arcuatus*

467 ▲ *P. annularis*

468 ▲ *P. asfur*

469 ▲ *P. chrysurus*

470 ▲ *P. imperator*

471 ▲ *P. maculosus*

472 ▲ *P. (Euxiphipops) navarchus*

473 ▲ *P. (Euxiphipops) sexstriatus*

474 ▲ *P. (Euxiphipops) xanthometopon*

475 ▲ *P. semicirculatus*

476 ▲ *P. striatus*

477 ▲ *P. zonipectus*

Hybridization (Crossings) in Butterfly and Angelfishes

Few marine fish hybrids have been reported; for example, Slasteneko (1957) listed 212 known fish hybrids and all but 30 of them were freshwater. Feddern (1968) was the first to document this phenomenon in marine angelfishes. He reported a cross between *Holacanthus ciliaris* and *H. isabelita* (now regarded as *H. bermudensis*). More recently, Randall et al. (1977) discussed hybridization in butterflyfishes. A total of 16 hybrid crosses (see table below) has been observed so far — 11 involving butterflyfishes and five with angelfishes.

It is interesting to speculate on the circumstances under which hybridization among chaetodontids and pomacanthids might occur. In a study of western Pacific butterflyfishes by Reese (1975) it was noted that some species characteristically occur in permanent pairs, whereas others are solitary or form aggregations. Most of the butterflyfishes and angelfishes that are known to hybridize belong to solitary or pair-forming species. It seems likely, then, that hybridization occurs in situations in which conspecific mates are in short supply. Thus an individual is forced to spawn with a closely related species; for example, at Christmas Island in the northeastern Indian Ocean the angelfish *Centropyge flavissimus* is abundant and *C. eibli* is scarce. In the absence of a suitable mate it is not difficult to envisage that *C. eibli* might be attracted to *C. flavissimus* during reproductive periods. Indeed, on a recent expedition to this locality Roger Steene and I collected a hybrid between these species.

An obvious prerequisite for hybridization is a close phylogenetic relationship between the interbreeding species. Of the crosses listed below only three *(kleinii* x *unimaculatus, miliaris* x *tinkeri,* and *auriga* x *lunula)* involve members of different subgenera. In nearly every case the parental species share a strikingly similar morphology, although the color patterns may be very different.

Hybridization is, of course, widespread throughout the animal and plant kingdoms. The psittaciform birds or parrots which might be regarded as the terrestrial counterpart of the butterflyfishes and angelfishes exhibit a multitude of dazzling color patterns and are distributed primarily in the tropics. The species inhabiting Australia are among the most ecologically diverse and have been well documented. Hybridization in Australian parrots is widespread both in captivity and in the wild. Of the 52 species that inhabit the island continent all but 16 are known to form hybrids. Most of the interbreeding occurs between closely related forms, but in a few cases members of different genera have been involved.

A list of the known butterflyfish and angelfish hybrids is presented in the table that follows. In addition, Moe (1976) reported a cross between the Grey Angelfish *(Pomacanthus arcuatus)* and the French Angelfish *(P. paru)* which was produced under laboratory conditions.

Chaetodontidae

Chaetodon auriga x *C. ephippium* (Tuamotu Archipelago)
C. ephippium x *C. semeion* (Marshall Islands)
C. kleinii x *C. unimaculatus* (Marshall Islands)
C. miliaris x *C. tinkeri* (Hawaiian Islands)
C. aureofasciatus x *C. rainfordi* (Great Barrier Reef)
C. ornatissimus x *C. meyeri* (Palau Islands)
C. pelewensis x *C. punctatofasciatus* (Great Barrier Reef)
C. punctatofasciatus x *C. guttatissimus* (Christmas Island)
C. ephippium x *C. xanthocephalus* (Sri Lanka)
C. auriga x *C. lunula* (Hawaii and Western Australia)
C. miliaris x *C. multicinctus* (Hawaiian Islands)

Pomacanthidae

Centropyge eibli x *C. flavissimus* (Christmas Island)
Centropyge vroliki x *C. flavissimus* (Marshall Islands)
Holacanthus ciliaris x *H. bermudensis* (West Indies)
Pomacanthus chrysurus x *P. maculosus* (Kenya)
Pomacanthus xanthometopon x *P. sexstriatus* (Great Barrier Reef)

478.
Chaetodon tinkeri x
Chaetodon miliaris
SL 40 mm (1.6 in.);
TL 50 mm (2 in.).
Makua, Oahu, Hawaiian Islands.
Photo: Randall.

479.
Chaetodon ephippium
x *Chaetodon semeion*
Marshall Islands.
Photo: Nate Bartlett.

480.
Chaetodon miliaris x
*Chaetodon
multicinctus*
10 cm (4 in.).
Photo: Norman.

478 ▲

479 ▲

480 ▲   482 ▼   481 ▲   483 ▼

481.
Centropyge flavissimus
x *Centropyge eibli*
70 mm SL (3 in.).
Christmas Island (Indian Ocean), at a
depth of 18 m (59 ft).
Photo: Allen.
482.
Chaetodon kleinii x
Chaetodon unimaculatus
Photo: Randall.
483.
*Centropyge
flavissimus* x
Centropyge vroliki
A color variation
which differs from the
hybrid of the species
featured in Vol. 1
(page 110).
Photo: Baensch.

The Rearing of Butterfly and Angelfishes in the Aquarium

by Hans A. Baensch (Translated from German)

The aquarist who wants to rear marine fishes must be consistent in caring for them. This is particularly true for the rearing of chaetodontids and pomacanthids. Because of the beauty and the rich color of these fishes a hobbyist is easily induced to buy them without knowing anything about their proper rearing. A beginner is advised not to try these families before having gained some experience with other, more easily reared marine fishes. Moreover, before buying butterfly or angelfishes, one should also be able to cultivate green algae (Caulerpa). These algae represent a very useful indicator of good water quality, which is the basis for the successful rearing of these delicate and precious fish families. Only if the aquarist is fully conversant with salt-water chemistry, with the cultivation of green algae, and with the proper treatment of the most frequent diseases, will his efforts at rearing angelfishes turn out successful and rewarding. What àre the difficulties in keeping butterfly and angelfishes alive over a longer period? Coral fishes, in contrast to most of the fresh water species, live under very stable conditions. In the tropical habitats of fresh water fishes density, temperature, and pH-value of the water, and availability of food continuously change according to the season, whereas marine fishes enjoy, day by day, the same optimal conditions, unless the water is troubled by storms. Thus the main problem for the aquarist consists of creating and maintaining those constant water conditions.

The difficulties in the marine tank:
The water vaporizes – the density increases. The fishes breathe – the pH-value drops because of the overproduction of carbon dioxide as there are rarely plants in a marine tank that absorb CO_2. In a marine tank the absence of plants will increase the amount of nitrate faster than in a fresh water tank. The natural break down of ammonia is disturbed if a copper drug is used to treat diseases. In marine tanks without a biological filter the water can easily turn poisonous, because of the high pH-value of

8.3 – 8.5. In this range the ammonia, derived from excrement and leftover food is three times as poisonous as the ammonium in most fresh water tanks, where the pH-value does not exceed 7.5. Ammonium (NH_4), having bigger molecules than ammonia (NH_3), is not capable of penetrating the cell membranes of the fish's body and thus is regarded as non-poisonous. The higher the pH-value the bigger is the danger that non-poisonous ammonium (NH_4) changes into poisonous ammonia (NH_3). The different salts in saltwater give it a pH range of 8.3 – 8.5. This range is wholesome to marine fishes and should be used in the tank. The aquarist has to prevent all kinds of putrefying material from turning poisonous. The most important measures are a reasonable feeding (three small portions a day) and a good skimmer as a chemo-technical aid. In rearing butterfly and angelfishes a motor-driven skimmer is a must. Its costs are less than the costs of the two or three precious specimens you might lose without one. The installation of a skimmer will reduce the risk of losses for years. It goes without saying that such a skimmer needs careful attendance: it must be emptied daily.

The air and eventually the ozone supply must frequently be controlled and, if necessary, regulated according to experience or directions for use.

As already pointed out consistent care is the main principle for all successful rearing of coralfishes. Offences against the rules of correct rearing will create problems immediately, in most cases within a few hours or days, whereas in a fresh water tank ill-treatment might inflict damage only after weeks. Another most important point deals with the correct number of specimens occupying one tank: The restriction to only a few individuals is the secret of succesful rearing of marine animals. Two or three butterflyfishes or one larger angelfish per 100 liters (25 gal.) of water is enough. As a basic rule 5 to 10 cm (2 to 4 in.) of fish can be kept in 100 liters (25 gal.) of water if an excellent biological filtration system is used. The filtration can take place in the bottom (with coral sand raising the pH-value) and/or in a large outside filter. A slow filter should in any case be used on the bottom to provide biological cleaning of the water.

The required efficiency of the filter depends on the size of the tank.

The outside filter should be powerful enough to pump through the contents of the tank twice an hour, that is, for a tank of 500 liters (125 gal.) a filter-pump with a capacity of 1000 liters (250 gal.) per hour is needed. That seems quite powerful, but it is chosen with normally too densely populated aquariums in mind. Less populated tanks on the other hand require a pump of only half the capacity. Moreover, one should bear in mind that the efficiency of the filter will decrease within a few days as the pores are swiftly choked up. The outside filter should be filled with some material that readily traps bacteria, such as coral debris, activated charcoal, or volcanic ashes.

The nitrosomas bacteria and nitrobacteria transform ammonia into nitrite or nitrate respectively. If these useful bacteria are stunted in their growth by adding copper chemicals (more than 0.2 mg $CuSO_4$ = copper sulfate per 100 liters [25 gal.] of water), the excrement will not be dissolved biologically. When the treatment of diseases is based on copper compounds, it is absolutely necessary to add fresh water every few days in order to remove the ammonia. However, tapwater may do harm to the butterfly and angelfishes, unless it is aged by allowing it to stand overnight or by adding appropriate chemicals. Thus it is preferable to keep diseased fishes in a separate quarantine tank without sand or coral on the bottom. Additionally, their food should be limited. Half of the water should be replaced every two or three days with freshly prepared saltwater and also the medication according to prescription. Newly bought specimens should immediately be put in quarantine. New fishes are nearly always ill, though it does not seem so at first sight. When buying fishes you should observe the following rules:

1) The breathing: the gills should not move more rapidly than 80 times per minute.

2) The fishes must not show any signs of disease.

3) The best size when buying is 4 to 8 cm (1.5 to 3 in.) for butterflyfishes and 4 to 10 cm (1.5 to 4 in.) for angelfishes.

484.
Aquarium, 3.6 ft long, on a bench which is covered with the same carpeting material as the floor. The power-filter is installed below the tank; all the other technical equipment such as aerator and UV-lamp are concealed behind a panel on left side. The aquarium is positioned between two windows and is illuminated by two hanging bulbs of 150 Watts each.
Photo: Baensch.

To repeat all the rules of correct rearing is not possible. As a cautious marine aquarist you will certainly not have bought butterfly or angelfishes unless you have gained enough experience with other marine fishes and have acquired some knowledge about water exchange, pH-control, density, temperature, and disease treatments. The feeding methods are described in the tables which follow on pages 322 to 331. Some important advice about the treatment of sick fishes refusing their food are pointed out below: marine fishes drink — in contrast to fresh water fishes. This fact should be made use of by adding soluble vitamins (about 10 ml per 100 liters [25 gal.] of water) to their water. Another important aid is the feeding of sick fish with fructose (no grape sugar!). 50 g (2 oz.) fructose are added to 10 liters (2.5 gal.) of aquarium water. Fructose has the advantage over grape sugar that it goes straight into the blood without making a detour through the possibly damaged liver.

The sick fish should be left in the treated water for 10 to 12 hours to absorb the fructose. This treatment can be repeated every few days until the fish starts eating again.

Explanation of the Tables — Hints for Feeding

Geographical distribution
The table includes all regions where the occurrence of the different species has been scientifically documented.

Depth Range
Here the author indicates the depth at which the fish is normally found. Young specimens are often encountered in water even shallower than 50 cm (1.6 ft) at low tide.

Temperature Range
○ 15–20° C (59–68° F). Only a few species are able to survive such low temperatures. Among these are *Chaetodon marleyi* of South Africa, up to Cape Town,

and species that live in deep waters, where temperatures are usually lower than at the surface.

◑ 21–24° C (70–75° F). This is rather a narrow range, requiring extra care for successful rearing. These species can be kept with species normally requiring higher temperatures than 24° C (75° F). But temperatures permanently higher than 24° C (75° F) will considerably shorten the lifespan of those fishes that normally live in greater depths or cooler ocean currents.

● 25–28° C (77–82° F) are the optimal temperatures for the fishes mentioned in this column. In most cases they can tolerate temperatures as low as 20–22° C (68–72° F), or as high as 28–30° C (82–86° F), if the oxygen supply is also increased. Thus an additional air diffuser should be put into the tank on hot summer days.

Primary Natural Food
The different columns indicate the species' primary diet in the wild and serve as a guide to what to feed the butterfly and angelfishes in the aquarium.

Corals
Butterflyfishes that in their natural habitat mainly feed on coral polyps will normally not survive for a long period in a tank. Exceptions are *C. lineolatus*, *C. oxycephalus*, *C. reticulatus*, *C. speculum*, *C. unimaculatus*, *C. zanzibariensis*, and *C. rafflesi* — the latter has already been kept in a tank for more than ten years.

The abovementioned species are marked with **3** in the table which refers to the level of difficulty, i. e., the amount of care the species requires in captivity. All the other coral eating species had to be marked with **4**; coral diet cannot be replaced by anything

485.
A 2000-liter aquarium (530 gal.) in which twelve different angelfishes are kept. Rivalries rarely arise when each fish has its own territory but are common if the tank is too small. This aquarium is biologically cleaned by a special drizzling algae-filter.
Photo: Baensch/Jungbluth.

else in the tank. Occasionally an individual fish gets accustomed to feeding stones, mysis, conch meat, etc. If such a coral eater has been obtained, every effort must be made to bring it to accept some kind of food.

Sponges and Tunicates

Sponges, like coral polyps, cannot be replaced by any other dietary items in the aquarium. Most of the angelfishes feeding on sponges, however, can sooner or later be accustomed to some substitute food. Here, too, a variety of different foods should be tried. Plant food, food stone, and fresh green algae are seldom refused. When the fish is kept under excellent water conditions and perhaps with another fish, (like a scat) that eats readily, then normally a healthy specimen will start to eat the substitute diet when it gets really hungry.

Crabs, Worms, Invertebrates

Fishes which mainly feed on this kind of diet can easily be fed in the aquarium. The main food for young specimens should be living artemia. Mysis and sometimes Enchytrae are the right substitute diet for adults; Tubiflex should be fed seldom because it causes constipation and slimy excrement.
Frozen food is recommended for all species, provided it is carefully thawed and offered three to five times a day in small portions. A great variety of food items is usually a good idea.

Plankton

Plankton-eating fishes mostly occur in schools. Some healthy specimens, kept as a school in a home aquarium, willingly accept live artemia, all sorts of frozen food, including finely chopped fish, beef, and prawns, flake food, and freeze-dried food. Live plankton is an excellent stimulant to get the fish accustomed to such food.

Algae

Procuring algae is one of the biggest problems for the aquarist. In an aquarium populated with algae-eating fishes, it is not possible to grow excessive amounts. Thus a second tank (or a third respectively besides a quarantine tank) is necessary to grow

algae on fist sized stones. Water free of nitrate and a fish population as small as possible enable the algae to grow abundantly. To make things easier it is advisable to "inoculate" the tank with algae-covered rocks from another tank or from the sea. As a substitute one may also offer different kinds of fresh greens such as lettuce (not treated with pesticides naturally!) or spinach (even frozen), chickweed and watercress. These should be scalded with boiling water if the fish will not accept them raw.

Omnivores

None of these species are hard to feed in an aquarium. Some good flaky food containing 40–50% protein will be acceptable as basic food, but some frozen food, algae and scalded lettuce, or a flaky diet based on vegetable matter with a maximum of 30% protein should also be given.
Butterfly and angelfishes roam about all day long in search of food. No species fills its stomach with one big catch as do fishes of prey. They take their meals in very small portions and this should be taken into consideration when feeding them. It is absolutely necessary to feed them frequently by offering small portions, which the fishes finish in two or three minutes.
An aquarist who is not able, for lack of time, to feed his pets twice in the morning, at noon and in the evening, should not try to rear fishes like butterfly and angelfishes.

Length of Fish

This column gives the approximate length of fully grown specimens in their natural habitat. In the aquarium animals will normally not reach their maximum length. This is especially true for those species attaining a length of 30 cm (12 in.). Such big specimens should not be kept under aquarium conditions unless a large tank of more than two meters (6.6 ft) in length is available. The smaller species whose maximum length is about 12 cm (4.8 in.) will in most cases reach this size in a tank.

Minimum Size of Tank

No data in regard to the dimensions of the tank is given, because the amount of living space provided is of greater importance. Thus the only measures given here are those in liters (US gallons). If you do not know the capacity of your aquarium, calculate: length x width x height (in cm) divided by one thousand equals liters; or length x width x height (in in.) divided by 231 equals US gallons.

Availability
The letters e, d, r, and 0 mark the degrees of difficulty in obtaining the different species.

e = These species can easily be obtained, as they occur in abundance. There are plenty of exporting firms in the Philippines, Sri Lanka, and the Caribbean areas which provide an ample supply to fish importers in America and elsewhere.

d = These species are fairly difficult to obtain as they are rarely seen in the aquarium trade.

r = These species rarely appear in the aquarium trade, as they also seldom occur in nature. Normally the rearing of these species should be left to public aquariums.

0 = These species have not yet been reared in the aquarium as far as the author knows, and they cannot be procured from commercial dealers, as they occur far from the normal "fishing grounds."

Grade of Difficulty, i. e. Amount of Care Required
The relative amounts of effort needed to rear the different species are given by the numbers 1, 2, 3, and 4, number 1 being easiest to rear.

1 = Wholly undemanding species do not exist among the butterfly and angelfishes. This number could only be given to fishes such as *Dascyllus trimaculatus, Scatophagus argus,* and some other easy fishes for beginners.

2 = These fishes are still fit for the beginning marine aquarist. Their food consists mainly of flake diet and occasionally of frozen items. They are quite undemanding as far as the quality of the water is concerned. The pH-value may range between 7.9 and 8.5. The proportion of nitrate should not exceed 200 mg/l (756 mg/gal.) and that of nitrite should not be higher than 0.4 mg/l (1,5 mg/gal).

3 = Most of the butterfly and angelfishes belong to this group. The necessary conditions for successful rearing are a fully functioning biological filter or a luxuriant growth of green algae, and few individuals per tank. The food should include living items twice a week, for example, mysis, and more often, frozen food such as brine shrimps and red gnat larvae. The pH-value may vary from 8.1 to 8.4. The proportion of nitrate should not exceed 80 mg/l (302 mg/gal.) and that of nitrate should not be higher than 0.2 mg/l (0,75 mg/gal.).

4 = This group should only be reared in public aquariums. These fishes must be regarded as extremely demanding. Their main food, living corals, cannot be replaced in the aquarium by any other diet. Moreover, these species rarely adapt to the water quality found in the normal aquarium. Diving readers who have had the chance to encounter these species on coral reefs will clearly understand why these fishes are among the world's most precious creatures and why they should enjoy every possible protection.

Table 1

Scientific Name

Scientific Name	Indian Ocean										Japan to Australia										Pacific Ocean										Atlantic Ocean							
	Red Sea	East Africa	South Africa	Seychelles	Mauritius/Réunion/Madagascar	Arabian Gulf	Sri Lanka (Ceylon)	Maldives	India	Thailand	Malaysia/Indonesia	Philippines	Taiwan	Ryukyu Islands	Southern Japan	New Guinea	Great Barrier Reef	Lord Howe Island	Western Australia	Southern Australia	Solomon Isl. to New Caledonia	Fiji Islands	Samoan Islands	Society/Tuamuto Islands	Pitcairn/Rapa*	Easter Island	Marshalls/Marianas/Gilberts	Hawaiian Islands	Marquesas Islands	Eastern Pacific	Gulf of Mexico	Florida	Bermuda	N. Caribbean Sea	S. Caribbean Sea	St. Helena/Ascension	Cape Verde Islands	West Africa
Family Chaetodontidae																																						
Amphichaetodon howensis																		X		X																		
Amphichaetodon melbae																														X								
Chaetodon aculeatus																																X	X	X				
Chaetodon adiergastos											X	X	X	X					X																			
Chaetodon argentatus												X	X	X	X																							
Chaetodon assarius																			X																			
Chaetodon aureofasciatus																X			X																			
Chaetodon auriga	X	X	X	X	X		X	X	X	X	X	X	X	X	X	X	X	X	X	X	X	X	X	X	R		X	X	X									
Chaetodon auripes												X	X	X	X																							
Chaetodon austriacus	X																																					
Chaetodon aya																																X	X	X				
Chaetodon baronessa											X	X	X	X		X	X				X	X																
Chaetodon bennetti		X	X	X			X	X	X	X	X	X	X	X	X	X	X				X	X	X	X	R		X											
Chaetodon blackburnii		X	X		X																																	
Chaetodon burgessi												X																										
Chaetodon capistratus																															X	X	X	X	X			
Chaetodon citrinellus		X		X	X		X	X	X	X	X	X	X	X	X	X	X				X	X	X	X			X	X	X									
Chaetodon collare							X	X	X	X	X	X																										
Chaetodon daedalma														X	X																							
Chaetodon declivis																													X									
Chaetodon decussatus							X	X	X	X	X																											
Chaetodon dichrous																																				X		
Chaetodon dolosus		X	X		X																																	
Chaetodon ephippium											X	X	X	X	X	X	X	X		X	X	X	X	X	R		X	X	X									
Chaetodon falcifer																														X								
Chaetodon falcula		X		X	X		X	X	X																													
Chaetodon fasciatus	X																																					
Chaetodon flavirostris																	X	X			X	X	X		X													
Chaetodon frembli																												X										
Chaetodon gardneri							X	X																														
Chaetodon guezei					X																																	
Chaetodon güntheri											?	X	X	X	X	X	X			X																		
Chaetodon guttatissimus		X	X	X	X		X	X	X	X																												
Chaetodon guyanensis																																		X	X			
Chaetodon hoefleri																																						X
Chaetodon humeralis																																						X
Chaetodon kleinii		X	X	X	X		X	X	X	X	X	X	X	X	X	X	X		X		X	X	X	X			X	X										
Chaetodon larvatus	X																																					
Chaetodon leucopleura	X	X		X																																		

*This information is based on investigations made by Dr. J. Randall (Bishop Museum, Honolulu) which have not been published yet.
R = Rapa only, P = Pitcairn only, X = both.

Temperature Range legend: ○ = 15–20°C; 59–68°F   ◑ = 21–24°C; 70–76°F   ● = 25–28°C; 77–82°F

Butterflyfishes

Depth Range in Meters (ft)	Temp. Range	Corals	Sponges and Tunicates	Crabs, Worms, and Invertebrates	Plankton	Algae	Omnivores	Unknown	Approx. Length of Fish, Adult, cm (in.)	Min. Size of Tank Liters (gal.)	Availability e–d–r–0	Grade of Difficulty 1–2–3–4	Page number	Common Name
10–50 (33–160)	◑							X	18 (7)	300 (80)	0	?	(59)	Lord Howe Coralfish
?	○							X	16 (6.5)	300 (80)	0	?	164	San Felix Butterflyfish
20–100 (66–330)	◑ ●			X					10 (4)	200 (50)	e	3	165	Caribbean Longsnout Butterflyfish
3–20 (10–66)	●	X		X					15 (6)	200 (50)	r	3	(12)	Philippine Butterflyfish
5–20 (16–66)	◑ ●						X		20 (8)	200 (50)	d	3	166	Asian Butterflyfish
3–40 (10–130)	◑						X		13 (5)	200 (50)	r	3	(13)	Western Butterflyfish
5–15 (16–50)	●	X							13 (5)	200 (50)	r	3	(14)	Golden-Striped Butterflyfish
3–20 (10–66)	●			X					23 (9)	150 (40)	e	3	167(15)	Threadfin Butterflyfish
?	◑ ●							X	20 (8)	150 (40)	r	3	168	Oriental Butterflyfish
2–15 (6.6–50)	●	X							13 (5)	200 (50)	r	4	169	Exquisite Butterflyfish
30–150 (100–500)	◑			X					15 (6)	200 (50)	0	?	170	Doubleband Butterflyfish
3–15 (10–50)	●	X							13 (5)	300 (80)	r	4	(16)	Triangular Butterflyfish
5–30 (16–100)	●						X		18 (7)	300 (80)	d	4	(18)	Bennett's Butterflyfish
?	●		·					X	13 (5)	250 (60)	r	3	171	Blackburn's Butterflyfish
40–75 (130–246)	●			X					14 (5.5)	200 (50)	0	?	172	Burgess' Butterflyfish
2–15 (6.6–50)	◑ ●			X					10 (4)	150 (40)	e	3	173	Foureye Butterflyfish
2–15 (6.6–50)	●			X		X			13 (5)	200 (50)	e	3	(20)	Speckled Butterflyfish
3–15 (10–50)	●	X		X					16 (6.5)	250 (60)	r	3	174	Collare Butterflyfish
?	◑						X		15 (6)	250 (60)	0	3	176	Wrought Iron Butterflyfish
15–30 (50–100)	●			X					12 (5)	300 (80)	0	?	177	Marquesan Butterflyfish
2–20 (6.6–66)	●			X		X			20 (8)	200 (50)	r	2	178	Indian Vagabond Butterflyfish
4–40 (13–130)	●			X					16 (6.5)	300 (80)	0	3	180	Hedgehog Butterflyfish
40–200 (130–660)	●						X		14 (5.5)	250 (60)	0	3	181	African Butterflyfish
5–15 (16–50)	●						X		20 (8)	300 (80)	e	3	(21)	Saddled Butterflyfish
10–150 (33–500)	◑			X					16 (6.5)	250 (60)	r	3	182	Scythe Butterflyfish
3–15 (10–50)	●						X		20 (8)	250 (60)	e	3	183	Saddleback Butterflyfish
2–25 (6.6–82)	●						X		25 (10)	300 (80)	d	3	184	Red Sea Raccoon Butterflyfish
2–20 (6.6–66)	●						X		20 (8)	250 (60)	r	3	(22)	Black Butterflyfish
4–65 (13–213)	◑						X		13 (5)	250 (60)	r	3	186	Bluestripe Butterflyfish
20–50 (66–160)	●						X		17 (7)	300 (80)	r	3	187	Gardiner's Butterflyfish
60–200 (200–660)	●			X					11 (4.5)	300 (80)	0	?	188	Guezei's Butterflyfish
5–40 (16–130)	◑						X		15 (6)	250 (60)	r	4	(23)	Günther's Butterflyfish
5–25 (16–82)	●						X		12 (5)	300 (80)	r	4	189	Spotted Butterflyfish
100–200 (330–660)	◑			X					12 (5)	300 (80)	0	?	190	Threeband Butterflyfish
5–35 (16–115)	●							X	20 (8)	250 (60)	0	3	191	Hoefler's Butterflyfish
2–40 (6.6–130)	○						X		18 (7)	300 (80)	d	3	192	East Pacific Butterflyfish
10–40 (33–130)	●						X		14 (5.5)	200 (50)	e	3	(24)	Klein's Butterflyfish
3–15 (10–50)	●	X							12 (5)	300 (80)	r	4	193	Orange-Face Butterflyfish
30–80 (100–260)	●						X		18 (7)	300 (80)	r	3	194	Somali Butterflyfish

Table 2

Scientific Name	Indian Ocean										Japan to Australia										Pacific Ocean										Atlantic Ocean							
	Red Sea	East Africa	South Africa	Seychelles	Mauritius/Réunion/Madagascar	Arabian Gulf	Sri Lanka (Ceylon)	Maldives	India	Thailand	Malaysia/Indonesia	Philippines	Taiwan	Ryukyu Islands	Southern Japan	New Guinea	Great Barrier Reef	Lord Howe Island	Western Australia	Southern Australia	Solomon Isl. to New Caledonia	Fiji Islands	Samoan Islands	Society/Tuamuto Islands	Pitcairn/Rapa*	Easter Island	Marshalls/Marianas/Gilberts	Hawaiian Islands	Marquesas Islands	Eastern Pacific	Gulf of Mexico	Florida	Bermuda	N. Caribbean Sea	S. Caribbean Sea	St. Helena/Ascension	Cape Verde Islands	West Africa
Chaetodon lineolatus	X	X		X	X		X	X	X	X	X	X	X	X	X	X	X	X	X	X	X	X	X	X				X										
Chaetodon litus																								X														
Chaetodon lunula		X	X	X	X		X	X	X	X	X	X	X	X	X	X	X	X	X	X	X	X	X	X			X	X	X									
Chaetodon madagascariensis		X	X	X	X		X	X																														
Chaetodon marcellae																																					X	X
Chaetodon marleyi			X																																			
Chaetodon melannotus	X	X		X	X		X	X	X	X	X	X	X	X	X	X	X	X	X		X	X	X	X				X										
Chaetodon melapterus				X		X																																
Chaetodon mertensii											X	X	X	X		X	X	X			X	X	X	X	R		X											
Chaetodon mesoleucos	X																																					
Chaetodon meyeri		X	X	X			X	X	X	X	X	X	X				X	X	X		X							X										
Chaetodon miliaris																												X										
Chaetodon mitratus				X				X			Cocos-Keeling and Christmas is.																											
Chaetodon modestus												X		X	X	X			X								X	X										
Chaetodon multicinctus																												X										
Chaetodon nigropunctatus												X																										
Chaetodon nippon												X	X	X	X																							
Chaetodon ocellatus																															X	X	X	X	X			
Chaetodon ocellicaudus		X									X	X					X																					
Chaetodon octofasciatus												X		X	X	X	X	X	X	X																		
Chaetodon ornatissimus												X		X	X	X	X	X	X	X	X	X	X	X			X	X	X									
Chaetodon oxycephalus												X				X	X		X																			
Chaetodon paucifasciatus	X																																					
Chaetodon pelewensis														X	X	X					X	X	X	X				X										
Chaetodon plebeius								X			X	X	X	X	X	X	X	X	X		X	X																
Chaetodon punctatofasciatus											X	X	X	X	X	X	X		X		X							X										
Chaetodon quadrimaculatus															X								X	X	P		X	X	X									
Chaetodon rafflesi							X				X	X	X	X	X	X	X	X	X		X	X	X	X														
Chaetodon rainfordi																X	X	X																				
Chaetodon reticulatus											X	X	X	X	X	X					X	X	X	X	P		X	X										
Chaetodon robustus																																					X	X
Chaetodon sanctaehelenae																																				X		
Chaetodon sedentarius																															X	X		X	X			
Chaetodon selene											X	X	X	X	X	X																						
Chaetodon semeion								X			X	X	X	X		X	X				X	X	X	X				X										
Chaetodon semilarvatus	X																																					
Chaetodon smithi																									X													
Chaetodon speculum				X							X	X	X	X	X	X	X	X	X																			
Chaetodon striatus																																X	X	X	X			
Chaetodon tinkeri																												X										

Depth Range in Meters (ft)	Temperature Range	Corals	Sponges and Tunicates	Crabs, Worms, and Invertebrates	Plankton	Algae	Omnivores	Unknown	Approximate Length of Fish, Adult, in Nature cm (in.)	Minimum Size of Tank Volume in Liters (approx. gal.)	Availability e–d–r–0	Grade of Difficulty 1–2–3–4	Page number	Common Name
10–40 (33–130)	●	X					X		30 (12)	400 (100)	e	2	(25)	Lined Butterflyfish
1–25 (3.3–82)	◐						X		15 (6)	?	0	?	195	Easter Island Butterflyfish
1–30 (3.3–100)	●						X		18 (7)	250 (60)	e	2	(26)	Raccoon Butterflyfish
10–40 (33–130)	●						X		14 (5.5)	250 (60)	e	3	196	Madagascar Butterflyfish
35–95 (115–311)	○	X		X					14 (5.5)	250 (60)	r	4	198	Marcella Butterflyfish
1–120 (3.3–393)	○						X		18 (7)	250 (60)	r	3	199	South African Butterflyfish
3–15 (10–50)	●	X							15 (6)	250 (60)	e	3	(28)	Black-Backed Butterflyfish
3–20 (10–66)	●	X							12 (5)	250 (60)	r	4	200	Arabian Butterflyfish
10–40 (33–130)	●						X		13 (5)	250 (60)	e	3	(30)	Merten's Butterflyfish
5–30 (16–100)	●							X	16 (6.5)	250 (60)	r	3	202	White-Face Butterflyfish
5–25 (16–82)	●	X							20 (8)	400 (100)	e	4	(31)	Meyer's Butterflyfish
1–250 (3.3–820)	◐						X		13 (5)	250 (60)	d	3	204	Lemon Butterflyfish
30–70 (100–230)	●			X					14 (5.5)	300 (80)	0	?	206	Indian Butterflyfish
20–200 (66–660)	◐			X					17 (7)	300 (80)	0	?	208	Brown-Banded Butterflyfish
5–30 (16–100)	◐						X		12 (5)	250 (60)	r	3	209	Multiband Butterflyfish
3–15 (10–50)	◐	X							13 (5)	250 (60)	r	4	210	Black-Spotted Butterflyfish
5–20 (16–66)	◐●							X	15 (6)	250 (60)	r	3	211	Japanese Butterflyfish
2–20 (6.6–66)	◐●						X		16 (6.5)	300 (80)	e	3	212	Spotfin Butterflyfish
3–15 (10–50)	●	X							14 (5.5)	250 (60)	r	3	214	Spot-Tail Butterflyfish
3–20 (10–66)	●	X							10 (4)	300 (80)	r	4	(32)	Eight-Banded Butterflyfish
5–25 (16–82)	●	X							18 (7)	400 (100)	r	4	(33)	Ornate Butterflyfish
10–40 (33–130)	●	X							25 (10)	300 (80)	r	3	215	Spot-Nape Butterflyfish
4–30 (13–100)	●						X		14 (5.5)	250 (60)	r	3	216	Red-Back Butterflyfish
10–30 (33–100)	●						X		13 (5)	200 (50)	d	3	(34)	Dot-and-Dash Butterflyfish
3–20 (10–66)	●	X							10 (4)	400 (100)	d	4	(35)	Blue-Spot Butterflyfish
5–30 (16–100)	●						X		9 (3.5)	250 (60)	d	3	(36)	Spot-Banded Butterflyfish
2–15 (6.6–50)	●	X							16 (6.5)	300 (80)	r	4	218	Fourspot Butterflyfish
3–15 (10–50)	●	X		X					15 (6)	250 (60)	d	3	(38)	Latticed Butterflyfish
3–15 (10–50)	●	X							13 (5)	300 (80)	r	4	(39)	Rainford's Butterflyfish
5–20 (16–66)	●	X							15 (6)	250 (60)	d	3	(40)	Reticulated Butterflyfish
1–50 (3.3–160)	◐●							X	17 (7)	250 (60)	0	?	219	Robust Butterflyfish
2–20 (6.6–66)	●						X		15 (6)	300 (80)	0	?	220	St. Helena Butterflyfish
15–40 (50–130)	●			X					15 (6)	200 (50)	e	3	222	Reef Butterflyfish
10–50 (33–160)	●						X		10 (4)	250 (60)	r	3	(42)	Yellow-Dotted Butterflyfish
5–25 (16–82)	●						X		26 (10.5)	250 (60)	r	3	(43)	Dotted Butterflyfish
4–20 (13–66)	●							X	30 (12)	300 (80)	e	3	223	Golden Butterflyfish
10–30 (33–100)	◐							X	17 (7)	300 (80)	0	?	226	Smith's Butterflyfish
3–20 (10–66)	●	X							15 (6)	200 (50)	e	3	(44)	Oval-Spot Butterflyfish
3–20 (10–66)	●			X					16 (6.5)	250 (60)	e	2	228	Banded Butterflyfish
40–75 (130–246)	◐			X					15 (6)	250 (60)	r	3	230	Tinker's Butterflyfish

Table 3

Distribution

Scientific Name	Indian Ocean										Japan to Australia										Pacific Ocean										Atlantic Ocean							
	Red Sea	East Africa	South Africa	Seychelles	Mauritius/Réunion/Madagascar	Arabian Gulf	Sri Lanka (Ceylon)	Maldives	India	Thailand	Malaysia/Indonesia	Philippines	Taiwan	Ryukyu Islands	Southern Japan	New Guinea	Great Barrier Reef	Lord Howe Island	Western Australia	Southern Australia	Solomon Isl. to New Caledonia	Fiji Islands	Samoan Islands	Society/Tuamuto Islands	Pitcairn/Rapa*	Easter Island	Marshalls/Marianas/Gilberts	Hawaiian Islands	Marquesas Islands	Eastern Pacific	Gulf of Mexico	Florida	Bermuda	N. Caribbean Sea	S. Caribbean Sea	St. Helena/Ascension	Cape Verde Islands	West Africa
Chaetodon triangulum		X		X			X	X	X	X	X																											
Chaetodon trichrous																								X					X									
Chaetodon tricinctus																		X																				
Chaetodon trifascialis	X	X	X	X	X		X	X	X	X	X	X	X	X	X	X	X	X			X	X	X	X	R		X	X										
Chaetodon trifasciatus		X		X	X		X	X	X	X	X	X	X	X	X	X	X	X	X	X	X	X	X	X	R		X	X										
Chaetodon ulietensis											X	X	X	X	X	X	X		X		X	X	X	X			X											
Chaetodon unimaculatus		X	X	X	X		X	X	X	X	X	X	X	X	X	X	X	X	X	X	X	X	X	X			X	X	X									
Chaetodon vagabundus	X	X	X	X	X		X	X			X	X	X	X	X	X	X	X			X	X	X	X			X											
Chaetodon wiebeli											X	X	X	X	X	X																						
Chaetodon xanthocephalus		X	X	X	X		X	X																														
Chaetodon xanthurus											X	X	X	X																								
Chaetodon zanzibariensis		X		X	X																																	
Chelmon marginalis																	X		X																			
Chelmon mülleri																	X																					
Chelmon rostratus		X		X			X				X	X	X	X			X	X			X																	
Chelmonops truncatus																				X																		
Coradion altivelis															X		X																					
Coradion chrysozonus											X	X	X	X			X		X																			
Coradion melanopus											X						X																					
Forcipiger flavissimus	X	X	X	X	X		X	X	X	X	X	X	X	X	X	X	X	X	X	X	X	X	X	X	X	X	X	X	X	X								
Forcipiger longirostris			X														X		X					X	P		X	X										
Hemitaurichthys multispinosus																									P													
Hemitaurichthys polylepis											X	X	X	X	X	X	X	X			X	X	X	X	P				X									
Hemitaurichthys thompsoni																													X									
Hemitaurichthys zoster		X	X	X	X		X	X	X																													
Heniochus acuminatus		X	X	X	X	X	X	X	X	X	X	X	X	X	X	X	X	X	X	X	X	X	X	X			X											
Heniochus chrysostomus											X	X	X	X	X	X	X		X		X	X	X	X	P		X											
Heniochus diphreutes	X		X				X	X							X				X	X								X										
Heniochus intermedius	X																																					
Heniochus monoceros		X	X	X	X		X	X			X	X	X	X	X	X	X				X	X	X	X			X											
Heniochus pleurotaenia							X	X		X	X																											
Heniochus singularius											X	X	X	X	X	X	X		X								X											
Heniochus varius											X	X	X	X	X	X	X		X		X	X	X															
Johnrandallia nigrirostris																														X								
Parachaetodon ocellatus							X			X	X	X	X	X		X	X		X		X	X																

Depth Range in Meters (ft)	Temperature Range ○15–20°C;59–68°F ◐21–24°C;70–76°F ●25–28°C;77–82°F	Dominant Natural Food							Approximate Length of Fish, Adult, in Nature cm (in.)	Minimum Size of Tank Volume in Liters (approx. gal.)	Availability e – d – r – o	Grade of Difficulty i.e. Amount of Care Required 1 – 2 – 3 – 4	Page number (Those in Parentheses Refer to Vol. 1)	Common Name
		Corals	Sponges and Tunicates	Crabs, Worms, and Invertebrates	Plankton	Algae	Omnivores	Unknown						
3–15 (10-50)	●	X							15 (6)	300 (80)	d	4	231	Triangular Butterflyfish
3–25 (10-82)	●							X	12 (5)	250 (60)	r	4	232	Tahiti Butterflyfish
3–15 (10-50)	◐	X							15 (6)	300 (80)	0	4	(46)	Three-Stripe Butterflyfish
3–20 (10-66)	●	X							18 (7)	300 (80)	e	4	(47)	Chevroned Butterflyfish
3–20 (10-66)	●	X							15 (6)	300 (80)	e	4	(48)	Red-Fin Butterflyfish
3–20 (10-66)	●						X		18 (7)	300 (80)	d	2	(50)	Pacific Double-Saddle Butterflyfish
5–25 (16-82)	●	X							20 (8)	250 (60)	d	3	233(51)	Teardrop Butterflyfish
3–30 (10-100)	●						X		23 (9)	200 (50)	e	2	(52)	Vagabond Butterflyfish
4–25 (13-82)	●							X	18 (7)	250 (60)	d	2	234	Wiebel's Butterflyfish
5–25 (16-82)	●						X		20 (8)	300 (80)	d	3	235	Yellowhead Butterflyfish
15–30 (50-100)	●						X		14 (5.5)	200 (50)	e	2	236	Yellow-Tail Butterflyfish
3–15 (10-50)	●	X							12 (5)	200 (50)	r	3	237	Zanzibar Butterflyfish
4–15 (13-50)	●			X					18 (7)	300 (80)	0	4	(56)	Margined Coralfish
4–20 (13-66)	●			X					20 (8)	300 (80)	0	4	(57)	Müller's Coralfish
3–20 (10-66)	●			X					20 (8)	250 (60)	e	4	(58)	Beaked Coralfish, Copper-Banded Butterflyfish
2–40 (6.6-130)	○			X					15 (6)	250 (60)	0	3	(60)	Talma
3–15 (10-50)	●						X		15 (6)	300 (80)	r	4	(62)	Highfin Coralfish
3–15 (10-50)	●						X		15 (6)	300 (80)	r	4	(64)	Orange-Banded Coralfish
3–15 (10-50)	●						X		13 (5)	300 (80)	r	4	(66)	Two-Eyed Coralfish
5–25 (16-82)	●			X					15 (6)	300 (80)	e	3	(68)	Long-Nosed Butterflyfish
5–25 (16-82)	●			X					19 (7.5)	300 (80)	r	4	338(69)	Big (Black) Long-Nosed Butterflyfish
30–50 (100-160)	◐ ●				X				20 (8)	400 (100)	0	?	238	Many-Spined Butterflyfish
5–40 (16-130)	●				X				18 (7)	400 (100)	d	3	(70)	Pyramid Butterflyfish
5–40 (16-130)	○				X				18 (7)	400 (100)	r	?	239	Thompson's Butterflyfish
5–40 (16-130)	●				X				16 (6.5)	400 (100)	e	2	240	Black Pyramid Butterflyfish
2–30 (6.6-100)	●						X		20 (8)	150 (40)	e	2	341(73)	Long-Fin (Common) Bannerfish
2–20 (6.6-66)	●		X						15 (6)	250 (60)	r	4	(74)	Pennant Bannerfish
3–200 (10-660)	◐ ●				X				15 (6)	200 (50)	e	2	341(75)	Schooling Bannerfish
3–20 (10-66)	●						X		18 (6)	250 (50)	e	2	242	Red Sea Bannerfish
3–20 (10-66)	●							X	23 (9)	300 (80)	d	3	(76)	Masked Bannerfish
3–20 (10-66)	●							X	18 (7)	300 (80)	d	3	244	Indian Bannerfish
3–25 (10-82)	●							X	25 (10)	250 (60)	d	3	(78)	Singular Bannerfish
3–25 (10-82)	●							X	18 (7)	300 (80)	d	2	(79)	Humphead Bannerfish
5–40 (16-130)	◐						X		16 (6.5)	250 (60)	r	3	245	Barberfish
3–50 (10-160)	●						X		17 (7)	250 (60)	d	3	(82)	Ocellate Coralfish

Table 4

Distribution — grouped as **Indian Ocean** (Red Sea, East Africa, South Africa, Seychelles, Mauritius/Réunion/Madagascar, Arabian Gulf, Sri Lanka (Ceylon), Maldives, India, Thailand); **Japan to Australia** (Malaysia/Indonesia, Philippines, Taiwan, Ryukyu Islands, Southern Japan, New Guinea, Great Barrier Reef, Lord Howe Island, Western Australia, Southern Australia); **Pacific Ocean** (Solomon Isl. to New Caledonia, Fiji Islands, Samoan Islands, Society/Tuamuto Islands, Pitcairn/Rapa*, Easter Island, Marshalls/Marianas/Gilberts, Hawaiian Islands, Marquesas Islands, Eastern Pacific); **Atlantic Ocean** (Gulf of Mexico, Florida, Bermuda, N. Caribbean Sea, S. Caribbean Sea, St. Helena/Ascension, Cape Verde Islands, West Africa).

Family Pomacanthidae

Scientific Name	Red Sea	East Africa	South Africa	Seychelles	Mauritius/Réunion/Madagascar	Arabian Gulf	Sri Lanka (Ceylon)	Maldives	India	Thailand	Malaysia/Indonesia	Philippines	Taiwan	Ryukyu Islands	Southern Japan	New Guinea	Great Barrier Reef	Lord Howe Island	Western Australia	Southern Australia	Solomon Isl. to New Caledonia	Fiji Islands	Samoan Islands	Society/Tuamuto Islands	Pitcairn/Rapa*	Easter Island	Marshalls/Marianas/Gilberts	Hawaiian Islands	Marquesas Islands	Eastern Pacific	Gulf of Mexico	Florida	Bermuda	N. Caribbean Sea	S. Caribbean Sea	St. Helena/Ascension	Cape Verde Islands	West Africa
Apolemichthys arcuatus																												X										
Apolemichthys guezei				X																																		
Apolemichthys trimaculatus		X	X	X	X		X	X			X	X	X	X	X	X	X		X		X			X														
Apolemichthys xanthopunctatus		·																					*Caroline and Line is.*															
Apolemichthys xanthotis	X																																					
Apolemichthys xanthurus				X			X	X	X																													
Centropyge acanthops		X	X		X																																	
Centropyge argi																																X	X	X	X			
Centropyge aurantius																X	X						X															
Centropyge aurantonotus																																			X			
Centropyge bicolor											X	X	X	X	X	X	X		X		X	X	X															
Centropyge bispinosus		X		X			X	X			X	X	X	X	X	X	X	X			X	X	X	X			X											
Centropyge colini													*Cocos-Keeling is.*																									
Centropyge eibli							X	X			X	X				X	X		X																			
Centropyge ferrugatus												X	X	X																								
Centropyge fisheri																												X										
Centropyge flavicauda											X	X	X	X	X	X	X				X	X	X	X														
Centropyge flavipectoralis				X																																		
Centropyge flavissimus																	X				X	X	X	X			X		X									
Centropyge heraldi													X	X	X		X				X				P		X											
Centropyge hotumatua																									X	X												
Centropyge interruptus															X																							
Centropyge joculator												*Cocos-Keel. and Christm. is.*																										
Centropyge loriculus																	X				X			X	P		X	X										
Centropyge multicolor																						X					X											
Centropyge multifasciatus											X	X				X					X	X	X	X														
Centropyge multispinis		X	X	X			X	X		X																												
Centropyge nigriocellus																								*Johnston and Line is.*														
Centropyge nox											X	X			X	X					X																	
Centropyge potteri																												X										
Centropyge resplendens																																				X		
Centropyge shepardi																											X											
Centropyge tibicen											X	X	X	X	X	X	X	X	X		X																	
Centropyge vroliki											X	X	X	X	X	X	X	X			X						X											
Chaetodontoplus ballinae																				X																		
Chaetodontopl. caeruleopunctatus												X																										
Chaetodontoplus chrysocephalus											X		X		X																							
Chaetodontoplus conspicillatus																				X	X																	
Chaetodontoplus duboulayi											X					X	X		X																			

Depth Range in Meters (ft)	Temperature Range ○15–20°C;59–68°F ◑21–24°C;70–76°F ●25–28°C;77–82°F	Corals	Sponges and Tunicates	Crabs, Worms, and Invertebrates	Plankton	Algae	Omnivores	Unknown	Approximate Length of Fish, Adult, in Nature cm (in.)	Minimum Size of Tank Volume in Liters (approx. gal.)	Availability e – d – r – 0	Grade of Difficulty i.e. Amount of Care Required 1 – 2 – 3 – 4	Page number (Those in Parentheses Refer to Vol. 1)	Common Name
														Angelfishes
12–50 (39–160)	◑		X						18 (7)	300 (80)	e	3	253	Bandit Angelfish
?	◑●							X	15 (6)	350 (90)	0	?	254	Réunion Angelfish
10–35 (33–115)	●		X						15 (6)	350 (90)	e	3	(92)	Three-Spot Angelfish
?	●		X						25 (10)	400 (100)	0	?	255	Golden Spotted Angelfish
10–25 (33–82)	●		X						15 (6)	300 (80)	r	3	256	Red Sea Angelfish
5–20 (16–66)	●		X						15 (6)	300 (80)	d	3	258	Indian Yellow-Tail Angelfish
15–50 (50–160)	●					X			7 (3)	100 (25)	r	2	259	African Pygmy Angelfish
30–70 (100–230)	◑●					X			6.5 (2.5)	100 (25)	d	3	260	Cherub Pygmy Angelfish
3–20 (10–66)	●							X	10 (4)	250 (60)	r	2–3	(94)	Golden Angelfish
15–200 (50–660)	●							X	6 (2.5)	100 (25)	r	2–3	261	Flameback Pygmy Angelfish
3–20 (10–66)	●					X			15 (6)	250 (60)	d	3	(95)	Bicolor Angelfish
10–50 (33–160)	●					X			8 (3)	150 (40)	d	3	(98)	Two-Spined Angelfish
50–100 (160–330)	●							X	8 (3)	200 (50)	0	?	262	Colin's Pygmy Angelfish
10–30 (33–100)	●					X			15 (6)	150 (40)	d	3	(100)	Eibl's Angelfish
10–30 (33–100)	●							X	10 (4)	200 (50)	d	3	263	Rusty Pygmy Angelfish
30–70 (100–230)	◑					X			6 (2.5)	150 (40)	r	3	264	Fisher's Pygmy Angelfish
10–60 (33–200)	●					X			6 (2.5)	150 (40)	r	3	(101)	White-Tail Angelfish
3–20 (10–66)	●					X			10 (4)	200 (50)	r	3	265	Yellowfin Pygmy Angelfish
2–15 (6.6–50)	●					X			9 (3.5)	200 (50)	e	3	(102)	Lemonpeel Angelfish
10–45 (33–148)	●					X			10 (4)	200 (50)	e	3	(103)	Herald's Angelfish
14–50 (46–160)	◑							X	8 (3)	200 (50)	0	?	266	Hotumatua's Pygmy Angelfish
15–60 (50–200)	◑					X			15 (6)	200 (50)	r	3	267	Japanese Pygmy Angelfish
15–70 (15–230)	●							X	9 (3.5)	200 (50)	0	?	268	Cocos Pygmy Angelfish
5–60 (16–200)	●				X				12 (5)	200 (50)	d	2	(104)	Flame Angelfish
20–60 (66–200)	●							X	9 (3.5)	200 (50)	0	4	269	Multicolor Pygmy Angelfish
20–70 (66–230)	●							X	10 (4)	250 (60)	r	3	(105)	Multi-Barred Angelfish
3–40 (10–130)	●					X			9 (3.5)	200 (50)	e	3	(106)	Many-Spined Angelfish
4–15 (13–50)	●					X			6 (2.5)	150 (40)	0	?	270	Black-Spot Pygmy Angelfish
10–40 (33–130)	●					X			9 (3.5)	300 (80)	e	3	(107)	Midnight Angelfish
10–50 (33–160)	◑					X			10 (4)	200 (50)	e	3	271	Potter's Pygmy Angelfish
15–40 (50–130)	◑●					X			6 (2.5)	150 (40)	r	3	272	Resplendent Pygmy Angelfish
10–56 (33–184)	●					X			12 (5)	250 (60)	0	?	273	Shepard's Pygmy Angelfish
4–30 (13–100)	●					X			18 (7)	350 (90)	e	2	(108)	Keyhole Angelfish
3–15 (10–50)	●					X			10 (4)	200 (50)	e	2–3	(109)	Pearl-Scaled Angelfish
?	◑		X						20 (8)	300 (80)	0	?	(112)	Ballina Angelfish
?	●		X						14 (5.5)	300 (80)	r	4	274	Blue-Spotted Angelfish
?	◑●		X						22 (9)	300 (80)	r	3	275	Orange-Faced Angelfish
?	●		X						25 (10)	400 (100)	r	4	(113)	Conspicuous Angelfish
5–20 (16–66)	●		X						25 (10)	300 (80)	r	3	(114)	Scribbled Angelfish

Table 5 — Scientific Name	Indian Ocean										Japan to Australia										Pacific Ocean										Atlantic Ocean							
Scientific Name	Red Sea	East Africa	South Africa	Seychelles	Mauritius/Réunion/Madagascar	Arabian Gulf	Sri Lanka (Ceylon)	Maldives	India	Thailand	Malaysia/Indonesia	Philippines	Taiwan	Ryukyu Islands	Southern Japan	New Guinea	Great Barrier Reef	Lord Howe Island	Western Australia	Southern Australia	Solomon Isl. to New Caledonia	Fiji Islands	Samoan Islands	Society/Tuamuto Islands	Pitcairn/Rapa*	Easter Island	Marshalls/Marianas/Gilberts	Hawaiian Islands	Marquesas Islands	Eastern Pacific	Gulf of Mexico	Florida	Bermuda	N. Caribbean Sea	S. Caribbean Sea	St. Helena/Ascension	Cape Verde Islands	West Africa
Chaetodontoplus melanosoma											X	X	X	X	X	X																						
Chaetodontoplus mesoleucus											X	X	X	X	X	X					X																	
Chaetodontoplus personifer													X						X	X																		
Chaetodontoplus septentrionalis											X	X	X	X	X																							
Genicanthus bellus											Cocos-Keeling is.													X														
Genicanthus caudovittatus	X	X			X																																	
Genicanthus lamarck		X									X	X		X	X	X					X																	
Genicanthus melanospilos											X			X		X	X				X	X																
Genicanthus personatus																												X										
Genicanthus semicinctus																		X																				
Genicanthus semifasciatus													X	X	X																							
Genicanthus spinus																									X													
Genicanthus watanabei											X	X	X			X					X			X	P													
Holacanthus africanus																																					X	X
Holacanthus bermudensis																															X	X	X	X				
Holacanthus ciliaris																															X	X		X	X			
Holacanthus clarionensis																														X								
Holacanthus limbaughi																														X								
Holacanthus passer																														X								
Holacanthus tricolor																															X	X	X	X				
Holacanthus venustus												X	X	X																								
Pomacanthus arcuatus																															X	X		X	X			
Pomacanthus annularis					X		X	X	X						X						X																	
Pomacanthus asfur	X																																					
Pomacanthus chrysurus		X			X																																	
Pomacanthus imperator	X	X	X	X	X	X	X	X	X	X	X	X	X	X	X	X	X		X		X	X	X	X	P		X	X										
Pomacanthus maculosus	X	X			X																																	
Pomacanthus navarchus											X					X			X																			
Pomacanthus paru																															X	X	X	X	X			X
Pomacanthus semicirculatus	X	X	X	X			X	X	X	X	X	X	X	X	X	X	X	X	X	X	X	X	X															
Pomacanthus sexstriatus											X	X	X	X		X	X		X		X																	
Pomacanthus striatus		X	X																																			
Pomacanthus xanthometopon								X			X			X		X	X																					
Pomacanthus zonipectus																														X								
Pygoplites diacanthus	X	X		X	X		X	X	X	X	X	X	X	X		X	X		X		X	X	X	X			X											

Depth Range in Meters (ft)	Temperature Range ○15–20°C;59–68°F ◑21–24°C;70–76°F ●25–28°C;77–82°F	Dominant Natural Food							Approximate Length of Fish, Adult, in Nature cm (in.)	Minimum Size of Tank Volume in Liters (approx. gal.)	Availability e – d – r – 0	Grade of Difficulty i.e. Amount of Care Required 1 – 2 – 3 – 4	Page number (Those in Parentheses Refer to Vol. 1)	Common Name
		Corals	Sponges and Tunicates	Crabs, Worms, and Invertebrates	Plankton	Algae	Omnivores	Unknown						
5–25 (16–82)	●		X						17 (7)	250 (60)	d	3	(116)	Black Velvet Angelfish
5–25 (16–82)	●		X						17 (7)	250 (60)	d	3	(117)	Vermiculated Angelfish
10–50 (33–160)	●		X						23 (9)	400 (100)	r	4	(118)	Yellow-Tail Angelfish
5–20 (16–66)	●		X						20 (8)	300 (80)	r	4	276	Blue-Stripe Angelfish
50–100 (160–330)	◑●				X				17 (7)	300 (80)	r	4	277	Ornate Angelfish
25–50 (82–160)	●				X				20 (8)	300 (80)	r	3	278	Zebra Angelfish
10–50 (33–160)	●				X				12 (5)	250 (60)	r	3	(127)	Lamarck's Angelfish
20–50 (66–160)	●				X				21 (8.5)	400 (100)	r	3	(128)	Black-Spot Angelfish
20–85 (66–279)	◑					X			21 (8.5)	400 (100)	r	3	280	Masked Angelfish
20–50 (66–160)	◑				X				18 (7)	400 (100)	r	3	(129)	Half-Banded Angelfish
15–100 (50–330)	●				X				20 (8)	400 (100)	r	3	281	Japanese Swallow
30–60 (100–200)	◑				X				35 (14)	500 (125)	0	?	282	Pitcairn Angelfish
30–50 (100–160)	●				X				15 (6)	300 (80)	d	3	(130)	Watanabe's Angelfish
2–40 (6.6–130)	◑●		X						45 (18)	500 (125)	r	3	284	West African Angelfish
2–60 (6.6–200)	◑●		X						45 (18)	500 (125)	e	3	286	Blue Angelfish
2–70 (6.6–230)	◑●		X						45 (18)	500 (125)	e	3	288	Queen Angelfish
5–70 (16–230)	◑		X						20 (8)	400 (100)	r	4	292	Clarion Angelfish
6–70 (20–230)	◑		X						25 (10)	300 (80)	0	?	294	Clipperton Angelfish
3–80 (10–260)	◑		X						25 (10)	400 (100)	d	4	295	King Angelfish
1–40 (3.3–130)	◑●		X						30 (12)	400 (100)	e	3	296	Rock Beauty
10–40 (33–130)	●							X	10 (4)	250 (60)	d	3	299	Purple-Mask Angelfish
2–40 (6.6–130)	◑●		X						50 (20)	500 (125)	e	3	300	Grey Angelfish
10–30 (33–100)	●		X						30 (12)	400 (100)	d	4	(132)	Blue-Ringed Angelfish
3–15 (10–50)	●		X						40 (16)	300 (80)	e	3	302	Arabian Angelfish
5–20 (16–66)	●		X						25 (10)	400 (100)	e	3	304	Ear-Spot Angelfish
3–70 (10–230)	●		X						30 (12)	500 (125)	e	3	(134)	Emperor Angelfish
4–20 (13–66)	●		X						30 (12)	500 (125)	d	3	306	Yellow-Band Angelfish
3–20 (10–66)	●		X						25 (10)	400 (100)	d	4	(120)	Blue-Girdled Angelfish
3–30 (10–100)	◑●		X						38 (15)	500 (125)	e	3	308	French Angelfish
5–30 (16–100)	●		X						40 (16)	500 (125)	e	3	(136)	Semicircle Angelfish
5–30 (16–100)	●		X						50 (20)	800 (200)	d	3	(121)	Six-Banded Angelfish
?	◑●		X						46 (18.5)	800 (200)	r	3	310	Old Woman Angelfish
5–20 (16–66)	●		X						38 (15)	500 (125)	d	4	(124)	Yellow-Faced Angelfish
6–35 (20–115)	◑		X						46 (18.5)	500 (125)	r	4	311	Cortez Angelfish
3–25 (10–82)	●		X						25 (10)	400 (100)	d	4	(138)	Regal Angelfish

Photographing Butterfly and Angelfishes in the Sea

(by G. R. Allen)

Many diving associates and others I have met on my travels have expressed an interest in the methods and equipment used for taking underwater photographs of fishes. Both Roger Steene, the author of Vol. 1, and I use similar techniques which I will briefly describe. A Nikon-F single-lens reflex camera is our choice, although there are several other excellent cameras on the market with similar capabilities. We selected the Nikon-F because of its wide range of accessories which includes a large action finder or viewing screen that is especially important for taking underwater photos. Another advantage of the Nikon system is the excellent 105-mm Micro-Nikkor lens which is the real key to obtaining high-quality fish portraits. Occasionally we use a 55-mm Micro lens; for example, when photographing a school of fishes, an exceptionally large fish, or diving in cool, temperate waters (temperate fishes are far less shy and can be approached at a much closer range than tropical species). The 105 mm lens, however, is the real "workhorse" and is used 95% of the time in tropical waters. It is extremely versatile for close-ups of subjects that range in size from juvenile butterflyfishes, damselfishes, and gobies to the larger angelfishes.

The camera is housed in a commercially manufactured underwater case. I use an aluminium housing made by Oceanic Products and Steene has the popular lightweight Ikelite constructed of transparent perspex. Both cases are made in the United States but similar models are available from European and Japanese manufacturers.

Both Steene and I use relatively simple strobe-lighting techniques that consist of a single inexpensive flash unit in a perspex underwater case mounted about 30 to 40 cm (12 to 16 in.) to one side or directly above the camera housing. The flash is fastened to a movable bracket which, depending on the distance, allows it to be tilted at different angles toward the subject. The flash unit is connected to the camera housing by a commercially manufactured lead which is well insulated. Because all photos are taken with a flash, the shutter speed is constantly kept at 1/60th second. We prefer Ektachrome ER film which is rated at ASA 64. The recommended F-stops for this film under average underwater conditions are as follows (lens to subject distance in parentheses): F−16 (25 to 30 cm; 10 to 12 in.), F−11 (35 to 45 cm; 14 to 18 in.), F−8 (60 to 80 cm; 24 to 32 in.), F−5.6 (90 to 120 cm; 36 to 48 in.). However, I never leave anything to chance and prefer to bracket at least one F-stop on either side of what I estimate to be the perfect setting. This often means much patient stalking of the subject and finally firing the shutter when the combination of focus, pose, and desired background come into synchronization. In underwater photography, like most other endeavors, there is no substitute for experience. Once you have the proper equipment it is a matter of practice. In some cases it may take several years before truly excellent results are obtained.

Text and Photo Supplement to Vol. 1

<u>Corrections Vol. 1</u>

p. 28   picture nos. 31 and 33 represent the juvenile of *C. ocellicaudus.*

p. 53   picture no. 77 illustrates a hybrid of *C. lunula* and *C. auriga.*

p. 59   *Chelmonops howensis* is now *Amphichaetodon howensis* according to Burgess (1978).

p. 124   *Euxiphipops xanthometapon* = *Pomacanthus xanthometopon*

The following supplementary section deals with nocturnal coloration and variations in pattern related to geography, age, and sex. Species appearing in this section were also featured in Vol. 1.

486.
Heniochus monoceros
An underwater photo from the coast of Kenya. The diving photographer should not hesitate to experiment with unusual angles.
Photo: Voigtmann.

Night Coloration of Butterflyfishes

487 ▲

487.
Chaetodon citrinellus
Night coloration.
Underwater photo,
Great Barrier Reef,
Australia.
Photo: Steene.

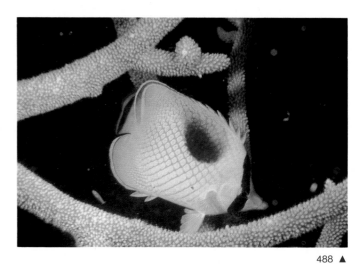

488 ▲

488.
Chaetodon rafflesi
Night coloration.
Great Barrier Reef,
Australia.
Photo: Steene.

489.
*Chaetodon
vagabundus*
Great Barrier Reef,
Australia.
Photo: Steene.

490.
Chaetodon lineolatus
Night coloration.
Coast of Kenya.
Underwater photo.
Photo: Kipper.

489 ▼

490 ▼

Chaetodon auriga

491.
Chaetodon auriga
Night coloration.
Coast of Kenya.
Photo: Kipper.

Juveniles of Butterfly and Angelfishes

492 ▲   494 ▼

493 ▲   495 ▼

496 ▼

492.
Chaetodon güntheri
6 cm (2.4 in.).
Aquarium photo,
Taiwan.
Photo: Shen.

493.
*Centropyge
flavissimus*
6 cm (2.4 in.).
This species has a
spot in the middle of
the body as a juvenile.
Photo: Steene.

494.
Vinculum sexfasciatum
6 cm (2.4 in.).
Photo: Steene.

495.
*Chaetodontoplus
melanosoma*
4.3 cm (1.7 in.).
Photo: Norman.

496.
*Apolemichthys
trimaculatus*
4.5 cm (1.8 in.).
The black margin on
the anal fin is just de-
veloping. At a length
of about 7 cm (2.8 in.)
the fish loses the
black spot on the
dorsal fin.
Photo: Baensch.

497.
*Chaetodontoplus
melanosoma*

SL 11.7 cm (4.6 in.);
TL 14.2 cm (5.6 in.).
This individual was
captured in the south-
west of Shikoku,
Japan. It differs significantly in color from
the fish in photo
no. 498. The different
pattern may be relat-
ed to sex or geogra-
phic variability.
Photo: Randall.

Sex Differences and Color Variations

497 ▲

498 ▲

499 ▼

500 ▼

501 ▼

498.
Chaetodontoplus melanosoma
This form was described by Bleeker as *Chaetodontoplus dimidiatus.*
Compare with fish shown on page 116 of Vol. 1. The specimen has a length of 18 cm (7 in.) and was photographed near the Moluccas.
Photo: Debelius.

499.
Pygoplites diacanthus
Underwater photo, Red Sea. Compare this photo with that shown in Vol. 1, pages 138–139. Red Sea individuals have an orange throat, whereas a blue throat is characteristic of Indo-Pacific fish.
Photo: Roediger.

500.
Chaetodontoplus personifer
Female SL 177 mm (7 in.); the specimen shown in Vol. 1, page 118, photo no. 175, is a male.
Photo: Shen.

501.
Genicanthus watanabei
This color variation from Taiwan was described by Shen and Liu as *Genicanthus vermiculatus.* See Vol. 1, page 130.
Photo: Shen.

Forcipiger longirostris
Black Long-Nosed Butterflyfish

BROUSSONET, 1782

502 ▲   503 ▼

The more common yellow color variety of this species was described in Vol. 1. Although *F. longirostris* has a broad distribution in the tropical Indo-West Pacific the dark phase is rarely seen. Most of the recorded observations and virtually all the live specimens originated from the Kona coast on the island of Hawaii; for example off the city of Refuge and at Kealakekua Bay a few individuals can be seen on nearly every dive. It has also been observed at the Society Islands, Great Barrier Reef, and recently at the Comore Islands and Christmas Island in the Indian Ocean. At the latter locality *F. longirostris* outnumbered the closely related *F. flavissimus* by a ratio of 2 : 1. Approximately one black individual was seen per 100 yellow phase fish. In addition, a rare intermediate variety was observed (see photo). The Black Long-Nosed Butterflyfish is generally found alone or in pairs, usually in the company of a yellow individual. Dark specimens kept in an aquarium will often transform to the normal yellow phase or will at least partly change color. This species is closely related to *F. flavissimus* but is distinguished by its longer snout length (see Vol. 1, p. 68 to 69). The maximum size is about 19 cm (7.6 in.).

A Natural Reef in the Red Sea as an example for aquarium decoration

502.
Forcipiger longirostris
This individual is in the first stages of transition to the black color form. Underwater photo taken at Christmas Island at a depth of 12 meters (39 ft).
Photo: Allen.

503.
Forcipiger longirostris at a length of 15 cm (6 in.). This photo was taken on the Kona coast (Hawaii), at a depth of 10 m (33 ft). The black (melanistic) form is relatively rare and represents a small percentage of the population.
Photo: Allen.

504.
Chaetodon melannotus
Adult browsing on corals on a reef along the coast of Kenya. Damselfishes, wrasses, cardinalfishes, and an orange fairy basslet are also evident in the photo.
Photo: Voigtmann.

An Extraordinary School of
Heniochus acuminatus, Maldive Islands

Photo: Voigtmann

Characteristics of *Heniochus acuminatus* and *H. diphreutes*

505.

These two species were treated in Vol. 1, but some readers have expressed a desire for more information concerning the differences between them. A scientific paper recently published by Allen and Kuiter (1978) explains these differences in detail. First the two species differ greatly in their ecology and general behavior. *H. acuminatus* is usually encountered alone or in pairs and is closely associated with the reef surface in areas in which there are living corals. *H. diphreutes,* on the other hand, is often found in large aggregations that feed on zooplankton well above the bottom; they retreat toward the substratum only when danger threatens. They are frequently inhabitants of relatively barren sandy areas where they congregate above isolated rock or dead coral outcrops. In addition, the two species differ in regard to several important morphological features:

Dorsal spines – *H. acuminatus* normally has 11 spines compared with 12 for *H. diphreutes.*

Fin proportions – The pelvic fins of *diphreutes* are significantly longer compared with those of *acuminatus*. The opposite, however, is true of the anal fin; in *acuminatus* the anal fin is larger than in *diphreutes* and there is also a difference as well in the shape of the anal fin; it is gently rounded in *acuminatus* and sharply angular in *diphreutes* (see drawings p. 342).

Head shape – The snout of *H. acuminatus* is more pronounced, and the ventral profile of the head of *diphreutes* has a "fuller" or more robust appearance (see drawings p. 342).

Maximum size – *H. acuminatus* attains a length of approximately 25 cm (10 in.), whereas *H. diphreutes* grows to about 15 cm (6 in.). There is also a difference in the minimum size of postlarval juveniles. The young of *H. acuminatus* first appear on inshore reefs at a size of approximately 15 mm (0.6 in.) standard length (from snout to tail base), whereas the smallest *H. diphreutes* are in the 25 to 30 mm (1 to 1.2 in.) range. *H. acuminatus* is widely distributed throughout the Indo-West Pacific but does not occur in Hawaii or the Red Sea. At these two localities it is replaced by *H. diphreutes,* which is also found in southern Japan, New South Wales, Western Australia, the Maldive Islands, and in the vicinity of Durban, South Africa. Both species can be observed during a single dive at certain localities off New South Wales, Australia.

Heniochus acuminatus
Long-Fin Bannerfish

Heniochus diphreutes
Schooling Bannerfish

506 ▲

506.
Heniochus acuminatus
This individual has an unusually long dorsal filament. Underwater photo from East Africa.
Photo: Roediger.
507.
Heniochus diphreutes

This species usually occurs in aggregations. The photo is from the Red Sea.
Photo: Schuch.

508.
Heniochus acuminatus
This species is usually found alone or in pairs

and on rare occasions in schools (photo on previous page). Underwater photo at the Abrolhos Islands, Western Australia.
Photo: Allen.

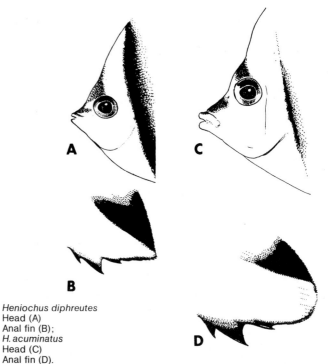

Heniochus diphreutes
Head (A)
Anal fin (B);
H. acuminatus
Head (C)
Anal fin (D).

507 ▼

508 ▼

Centropyge tibicen Spawning

509 ▲

509.
Centropyge tibicen
Pair. Miyake-jima,
Japan. The color differ-
ences of the sexes
can be seen clearly.
Female above and
male below.
Photo: Moyer.

510 ▼

510.
When spawning, the
pairs swim upwards
and eject their eggs
and sperm in the
open water. These re-
main visible as a
cloud over the fish
which are returning to
the bottom.
Photo: Moyer.

Further Reading on Butterflyfishes and Angelfishes

The following comprehensive list of the major works dealing with chaetodontids and pomacanthids includes literature cited in this volume. For the convenience of the reader this bibliography is divided into two sections, the first of which covers the general biology of butterflyfishes and angelfishes and the second treats their classification.

Biology of Butterflyfishes and Angelfishes and General Reading

Abel, E. R. 1960. Zur Kenntnis des Verhaltens und der Ökologie von Fischen an Korallenriffen bei Ghardapa (Rotes Meer). Z. Morphol. Ökol. Tiere, 49: 430–503.

Bauer, J. A., Jr. and G. Klay. 1974. Pigmy angels spawn. Octopus, 1 (5): 7–18.

Burgess, W. E. 1974. Une forme atypique de Chaetodon de Ceylon. Rev. fr. Aquariol., 2: 37–40.

Chlupaty, P. 1962. About the butterflyfishes of the genus Chaetodon. Trop. Fish Hobbyist, 11 (3): 42–47.

Debelius, H. 1976. Eine Erstvorstellung: Chaetodon arabicus (Steindachner). Das Aquarium, 84 (Juni): 261–263.

Ehrlich, P. R., F. H. Talbot, B. C. Russell, and G. R. V. Anderson. 1977. The behaviour of chaetodontid fishes with special reference to Lorenz's "poster colouration" hypothesis. J. Zool., Lond., 183: 213–228.

Feddern, H. A. 1968. Hybridization between the western Atlantic angelfishes, Holacanthus isabelita and H. ciliaris. Bull. Mar. Sci., 18(2): 351–382.

Fraser-Brunner, A. 1951. Pattern development in the chaetodont fish Pomacanthus annularis (Bloch), with a note on the status of Euxiphipops Fraser. Copeia, No. 1: 88–89.

Fricke, H. W. 1976. Bericht aus dem Riff. Piper-Verlag, München, W. Germany.

Graaf, Frank de 1977. Zwergkaiserfische. DATZ, 2 (Februar): 60–63.

Graaf, Frank de 1977. Zwergkaiserfische II. DATZ, 4 (April): 132–135.

Hamilton, W. J. III and R. M. Petermann. 1971. Countershading in the colorful reef fish Chaetodon lunula: concealment, communication, or both? Anim. Beh., 19(2): 357–364.

Hiatt, R. W. and D. W. Strasburg. 1960. Ecological relationship of the fish fauna on coral reefs of the Marshall Islands. Ecol. Monogr., 30: 65–127.

Hobson, E. S. 1965. A visit with el barbero. Underwater Nat., 3(3): 5–10.

Kerstitch, A. 1977. Butterflies and angels of the Sea of Cortez. Marine Aquarist (U.S.A.), 7(9): 17–28.

Lobel, P. S. 1975. Hawaiian angelfishes. Marine Aquarist (U.S.), 6(4): 30–41.

Mayland, H. J. 1976. Some Red Sea fishes. Marine Aquarist (U.S.), 7(5): 29–34.

Meyers, A. A. and P. M. Meyers. 1978. Rafflesi. Marine Aquarist (U.S.), 8(5): 42–45.

Miklosz, J. C. 1972. When is a koran not a koran? Marine Aquarist (U.S.), 3(4): 16–25.

Moe, M. A. Jr. 1976. Rearing Atlantic angelfish. Marine Aquarist (U.S.), 7(7): 17–26.

Moe, M. A. Jr. 1977. Inside the egg of an angelfish. Marine Aquarist (U.S.), 8(3): 5–12.

Moyer, J. T. and A. Nakazono. 1978. Population structure, reproductive behavior, and protogynous hermaphroditism in the angelfish Centropyge interruptus at Miyake-jima, Japan. Jap. J. Ichthyol., 25(1): 25–39.

Okuno, R. 1962. Intra- and interspecific relations of salt-water fishes in aquarium. I. Butterflyfishes. Japan. J. Ecol., 12(4): 129–133.

Randall, J. E. 1967. Food habits of reef fishes of the West Indies. Studies in tropical Oceanography No. 5. Univ. of Miami Inst. Mar. Sci.: 665–847.

Randall, J. E., G. R. Allen and R. C. Steene. 1977. Five probable hybrid butterflyfishes of the genus Chaetodon from the central and western Pacific. Rec. West. Aust. Mus., 6(1): 3–26.

Randall, J. E. and W. D. Hartman. 1968. Sponge-feeding fishes of the West Indies. Mar. Biol., 1(3): 216–225.

Reese, E. S. 1973. Duration of residence by coral reef fishes on "home" reefs. Copeia, No. 1: 145–149.

Reese, E. S. 1975. A comparative field study of the social behaviour and related ecology of reef fishes of the family Chaetodontidae. Z. Tierpsychol., 37: 37–61.

Reese, E. S. 1977. Coevolution of corals and coral feeding fishes of the family Chaetodontidae. Proc. Third Int. Coral Reef Symp. 1: 267–274.

Shen, S. C. and C. H. Liu. 1976. Ecological and morphological study of the fish fauna from the waters around Taiwan and its adjacent islands. 17. – A study of sex reversal in a pomacanthid fish Genicanthus semifasciatus (Kamohara). Acta Oceanographica Taiwanica Sc. Reports, Nat. Taiwan Univ. No. 6: 140–150.

Silner, L. 1965. Der Kaiserfisch von Akaba, Holacanthus (Apolemichthys) xanthotis – ein Neunachweis im Roten Meer. Neptun, 5: 246–247.

Slastenenko, E. P. 1957. A list of natural fish hybrids of the world. Hidrobiologi, ser. B, 4(2–3): 76–97.

Steene, R. C. 1977. Butterfly and Angelfishes of the World. Vol. 1, Wiley Interscience, New York.

Takeshita, G. Y. 1976. An angel hybrid. Marine Aquarist (U.S.), 7(1): 27–35.

TI Tatsachen und Informationen aus der Aquaristik 1977. 37 (März): S. 4–18.

Yasuda, F. 1967. Some observations on the color of the young forms of Chaetodontoplus septentrionalis (T. & S.). Sci. Rep. Yokosuka City Mus., 13: 78–81.

Yasuda, F. and Y. Tominaga. In press. Different color patterns of Holacanthus septentrionalis from the coastal waters of Japan. Jpn. J. Ichthyol.

Yasuda, F. and A. Zama. 1975. Notes on the two rare chaetodont fishes, *Parachaetodon ocellatus* and *Coradion chrysozonus* from the Ogasawara Islands. J. Tokyo Univ. Fish., 62(1): 33–38.

Zumpe, D. 1964. Laboratory observations on the aggressive behaviour of some butterfly fishes (Chaetodontidae). Z. Tierpsychol., 22(2): 226–236.

Zumpe, D. 1964. Kampfverhalten bei *Chelmon rostratus*. Die Aquarien und Terrarien Z., 17(7): 210–212.

Zumpe, D. 1964. Das Kampfverhalten bei *Heniochus acuminatus*. Die Aquarien und Terrarien Z., 17(10): 303–305.

Classification (Taxonomic Works)

References for every original description of the nominal species of butterflyfishes and angelfishes are not included. Most readers will not have a use for this information, but for students or professional ichthyologists who require it two basic references are recommended: Fraser-Brunner (1933) for the Pomacanthidae and Burgess (1978) for the Chaetodontidae.

Ahl, E. 1923. Zur Kenntnis der Knochenfischfamilie Chaetodontidae, insbesondere der Unterfamilie Chaetodontinae. Arch. Naturg. A 89(5): 1–205.

Allen, G. R. and R. H. Kuiter. 1978. *Heniochus diphreutes* Jordan, a valid species of butterflyfish (Chaetodontidae) from the Indo-West Pacific. J. Roy. Soc. West. Aust., 61(1): 11–18.

Allen, G. R. and R. C. Steene. 1979. The fishes of Christmas Island, Indian Ocean. Spec. Publ. Aust. and Nat. Parks and Wildlife, Canberra.

Baldwin, W. J. 1963. A new chaetodont fish, *Holacanthus limbaughi,* from the eastern Pacific. Los Angeles County Mus. Contri. Sci. No. 74: 1–8.

Böhlke, J. E. and C. G. Chaplin, 1968. Fishes of the Bahamas. Livingston Pub. Co., Wynnewood, Pennsylvania.

Burgess, W. E. 1973. *Apolemichthys xanthopunctatus,* a new species of angelfish (family Pomacanthidae) from the Pacific Ocean. Trop. Fish Hobbyist (U. S.), 21: 55–56, 86–89.

Burgess, W. E. 1974. *Centropyge aurantonotus,* a new species of pygmy angelfish from the southern Caribbean. Trop. Fish Hobbyist, 23 (225, No. 3): 90–97.

Burgess, W. E. 1978: A monograph of the butterflyfishes (Family Chaetodontidae). T. F. H. Publications, Inc., Neptune, New Jersey, U. S.

Burgess, W. E. and Axelrod, H. R. 1972. Pacific Marine Fishes. Book 2. TFH Publications Inc., Neptune, New Jersey.

Cuvier, G. 1831 (In: Cuvier, G. and A. Valenciennes). Histoire Naturelle des Poissons, Levrault, Paris.

Fraser-Brunner, A. 1933. A revision of the chaetodont fishes of the subfamily Pomacanthinae. Proc. Zool. Soc. London, 1933: 543–599.

Fraser-Brunner, A. 1950. *Holacanthus xanthotis,* sp. n. and other chaetodont fishes from the Gulf of Aden. Proc. Zool. Soc. London, 120: 43–48.

Freihofer, W. C. 1963. Patterns of the ramus lateralis accessorius and their systematic significance in teleostean fishes. Stanford Ichthyol. Bull. 8: 81–189.

Hubbs, C. L. 1963. *Chaetodon aya* and related deep-living butterflyfishes: Their variation, distribution, and synonymy. Bull. Mar. Sci., 13(1): 133–192.

Guézé, P. and L. A. Maugé. 1973. Redécouverte de *Chaetodon mitratus* Günther (Pisces: Chaetodontidae). Travaux et documents de l'O.R.S.T.O.M. communications présentées au Colloque Commerson La Réunion 16–24 Octobre 1973: 39–44.

Günther, A. 1860. Catalogue of the fishes in the British Museum. Vol. 2. Trustees Brit. Mus. (Nat. Hist.). London.

Klausewitz, W. 1963. *Centropyge eibli* n. sp. von den Nikobaren (Pisces, Percoidea, Pomacanthidae). Senck. biol., 44(3): 177–181.

Klausewitz, W. 1969. Vergleichend-taxonomische Untersuchungen an Fischen der Gattung Heniochus. Senckenbergiana biol. 50: 49–89.

Klausewitz, W. 1972. Litoralfische der Malediven. II. Kaiserfische der Familie Pomacanthidae (Pisces: Perciformes). Senck. biol., 53(5/6): 361–372.

Klausewitz, W. and T. Wongratana. 1970. Vergleichende Untersuchungen an *Apolemichthys xanthurus* und *xanthotis*. Senck. biol. 51(5/6): 323–332.

Lubbock, R. and R. D. Sankey. 1975. A new angelfish of the genus *Centropyge* (Teleostei: Pomacanthidae) from Ascension Island. Bull. Br. Mus. nat. hist. (Zool.), 28(5): 227–231.

Masuda, H., C. Araga and T. Yoshino. 1975. Coastal Fishes of Southern Japan. Tokai University Press, Tokyo.

Maugé, L. A. and R. Bauchot. 1976. Une espèce nouvelle de Chétodon de l'Océán Indien occidental: *Chaetodon guezei* (Pisces: Chaetodontidae). Bull. Mus. Natn. Hist. nat., Paris, 3rd ser., no. 355, Zoologie 248: 89–101.

Nalbant, T. 1964 (1965). Sur les Chaetodons de l'Atlantique, avec la description d'un noveau genere *Bauchotia* (Pisces: Chaetodontidae). Bull. Mus. Natn. Hist. nat., 36(5): 584–589.

Nalbant, T. 1973. Studies on chaetodont fishes with some remarks on their taxonomy (Pisces, Perciformes, Chaetodontidae). Travaux Mus. Hist. Nat. "Grigore Antipa" 13: 303–331.

Nalbant, T. 1974. Some osteological characters in butterfly fishes with special references to their phylogeny and evolution (Pisces, Perciformes, Chaetodontidae). Travaux Mus. Hist. Nat. "Grigore Antipa" 15: 303–314.

Ogilby, J. D. 1915. Review of the Queensland Pomacanthinae. Mem. Qld. Mus., 3: 99–116.

Randall, J. E. 1975. A revision of the Indo-Pacific angelfish genus *Genicanthus,* with descriptions of three new species. Bull. Mar. Sci., 25(3): 393–421.

Randall, J. E. 1975. Three new butterflyfishes (Chaetodontidae) from southeast Oceania. U O, 25: 12–22.

Randall, J. E. and D. K. Caldwell. 1973. A new butterflyfish of the genus *Chaetodon* and a new angelfish of the genus *Centropyge* from Easter Island. Contr. Sci. Los Angeles County Mus., no. 237: 1–11.

Randall, J. E. and W. Klausewitz. 1977. *Centropyge flavipectoralis,* a new angelfish from Sri Lanka (Ceylon). Senck. Biol., 57(4/6): 235–240.

Randall, J. E. and L. A. Maugé. 1978. *Holacanthus guezei,* a new angelfish from Réunion. Bull. Mus. natn. Hist. nat., Paris. 3rd Ser., no. 514, Zoologie 353: 297 – 303.

Randall, J. E. and P. J. Struhsaker. 1976. Description of the male of the Hawaiian angelfish *Genicanthus personatus.* Bull. Mar. Sci., 26(3): 414–416.

Randall, J. E. and R. C. Wass. 1974. Two new pomacanthid fishes of the genus *Centropyge* from Oceania. Jpn. J. Ichthyol., 21(3): 137–144.

Randall, J. E., and F. Yasuda. 1979. *Centropyge shepardi,* a new angelfish from the Mariana and Ogasawara Islands. Jpn. J. Ichthyol., 26(1): 55–61.

Shen, S. C. 1973. Ecological and morphological study on fish-fauna from the waters around Taiwan and its adjacent islands. 3. Study on the chaetodont fishes (Chaetodontidae) with description of a new species and its distribution. Rept. Inst. Fish. Biol. Nat. Taiwan Univ., 3(1): 1–75.

Shen, S. C. and P. C. Lim. 1975. An additional study on chaetodont fishes (Chaetodontidae) with description of two new species. Bull. Inst. Zool., Academia Sinica, 14(2): 79–105.

Shen, S. C. and C. S. Liu. 1979. Clarification of the genera of the angelfishes (family Pomacanthidae). Acta Oceanographic Taiwanica Sci. Repts. Nat. Taiwan Univ.: 57–77.

Smith, J. L. B. 1949. The sea fishes of southern Africa. Central News Agency, Ltd., South Africa.

Smith, J. L. B. 1955. The fishes of the family Pomacanthidae in the Western Indian Ocean. Ann. Mag. nat. Hist., (12) 8: 377–384.

Smith-Vaniz, W. F. and J. E. Randall. 1974. Two new species of angelfishes *(Centropyge)* from the Cocos-Keeling Islands. Proc. Acad. nat. Sci. Philad., 126(8): 105–113.

Tominaga, Y. and F. Yasuda. 1973. *Holacanthus interruptus,* a valid pomacanthid species, distinct from *Centropyge fisheri.* Jpn. J. Ichthyol., 20(3): 157–162.

Weber, M. and L. F. de Beaufort. 1936. The fishes of the Indo-Australian Archipelago, Vol. 8. E. J. Brill, Leiden.

Woods, L. P. and L. P. Schultz. 1953. Subfamily Pomacanthinae. In: Schultz, L. P. et al., Fishes of the Marshall and Marianas Islands. Bull. U.S. nat. Mus., 202(1): 597–608.

Yasuda, F. and Y. Tominaga. 1970. Two new long-tailed pomacanthine fishes from Miyake-jima and Okinawa-jima, Japan. Jpn. J. Ichthyol., 17(4): 141–151.

Yasuda, F. and Y. Tominaga. 1976. A new pomacanthid fish, *Chaetodontoplus caeruleopunctatus,* from the Philippines. Jpn. J. Ichthyol., 23(3): 130–132.

Index of Synonyms

Index of Common Names of Volumes 1 and 2

Page numbers up to 144 = Vol. 1; from 145 onward = Vol. 2

Index of Valid Scientific Names
in Volumes 1 and 2

Bold-faced type refers to the description and illustrations of the species. Page numbers up to 144 = Vol. 1; from 145 onward = Vol. 2.
Thin type refers to text dealing with generic or subgeneric classification.
No reference to the page numbers of the table (see pages 322 to 331) is made in this index.

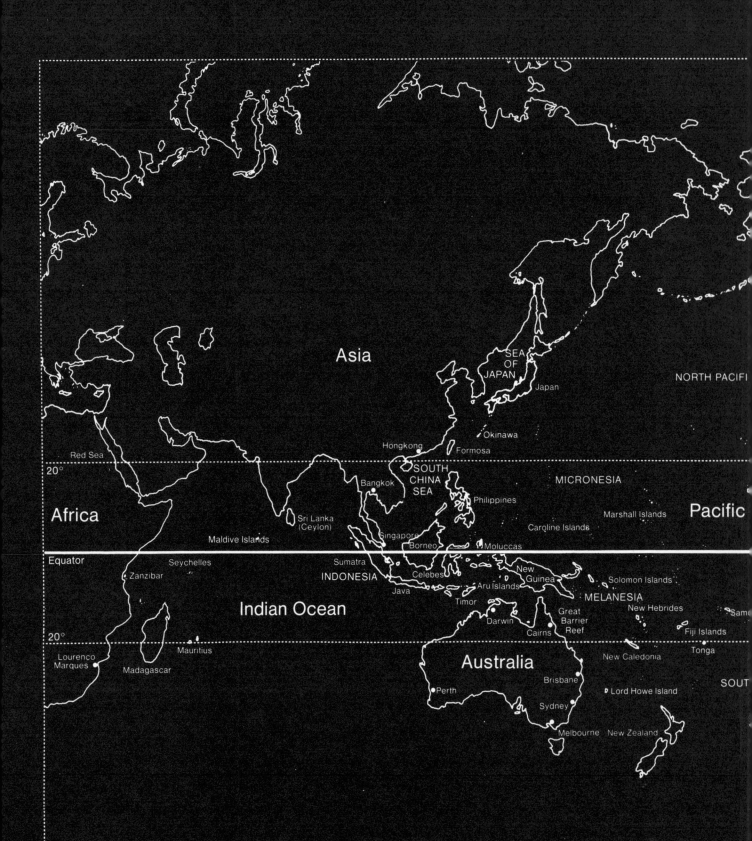